July 12, 2001

Dear Dennis,

Happy Birthday. Thank you for making our time in London very enjoyable. You will always be part of our memories of London.

Love

Michael, Brenda, Michael Jr & Katherine

London
from the Thames

London
from the Thames

Angelo Hornak

Little, Brown and Company

Boston · New York · London

A LITTLE, BROWN BOOK

First published in 1999
by Little, Brown and Company (UK)

Text and photographs
copyright © 1999 by Angelo Hornak

The moral right of the author
has been asserted.

A CIP catalogue record for this book is
available from the British Library

ISBN 1-85605-526-4

Designed by Andrew Barron and
Collis Clements Associates
Printed and bound in Italy by
L.E.G.O. SpA

Little, Brown and Company (UK)
Brettenham House, Lancaster Place
London WC2E 7EN

ACKNOWLEDGEMENTS

I would like to thank: Lesley Bossine of
Kew Bridge Steam Museum for help
with the history of the water supply;
Clive Cheesman, Rouge Dragon
Pursuivant at the College of Arms for
identifying the shields on Kew Bridge;
Colin Davis of the Port of London
Authority for help with the question of
transport on the river; John Cracknell,
Assistant Clerk to the Worshipful
Company of Fishmongers, for clarifying
the history of the Fishmongers'
Company; Jeremy Smith of the
Guildhall Library and Art Gallery for
locating black and white material; the
London Library for permission to
photograph and use material from their
shelves; Patrick Minns for a memorable
river trip; Jennie and her friends on
Houseboat Flamenco during the 1996
Boat Race; Clare Pemberton and Julia
Charles at Little, Brown for deciding to
risk publication; Linda Silverman for
undertaking the picture research;
Andrew Barron for his inspired design;
and last but by no means least my
editor Arianne Burnette for her
support, encouragement, patience and
skill. I am also grateful to my family for
putting up with my refusal to accept
any commitments 'in case it's the right
weather for a trip on the Thames'.

TECHNICAL NOTES

The colour photographs were taken on
a 6006 Rollei (medium format single-
lens-reflex camera system), with a
variety of lenses from 40mm to 250mm.
I used Fuji Provia film (100 and 400),
processed by Ceta in Clerkenwell.
My boat is an inflatable Zodiac 3.8m
Fastroller, powered by a 15hp Mariner
outboard.

The Upper Pool in 1844 (left).

Richmond Riverside, redeveloped in the
1990s (half-title page).

Tower Bridge at dusk (title page).

View of London by Visscher (endpapers).

Introduction

As a small boy growing up in Chelsea just after the war, I used to love walking down to the Thames to watch the boats, especially the coal barges delivering their loads to Battersea Power Station. Today the power station is closed, and the Thames is much quieter than it used to be. The river traffic in Chelsea is mostly confined to sightseeing cruises on their way to Kew and Hampton Court, police launches patrolling the river and regular bargeloads of London's rubbish on their way to landfill sites in Kent and Essex. There are also a few private pleasure craft, and I often thought what fun it would be to keep a boat on the Thames. Three years ago I realized this dream, and rented a mooring for a small boat at Cadogan Pier, on the very stretch of river that I used to visit as a child.

I decided to embark on a book of photographs of London from the Thames to coincide with the renewed interest in the river at the Millennium. As an architectural photographer I have always been fascinated by the great buildings that line the banks of the river and are seen at their best against a background of wide horizons and open skies, with a foreground of rippling and reflective water. A trip along the Thames takes in a wide range of building styles, from the Norman strength of the Tower of London to the Baroque magnificence of the royal buildings at Greenwich and Hampton Court. There are also examples of classical elegance at Somerset House and splendid Gothic Revival at Westminster and Tower Bridge. But the river is much more than a museum showcase for these historical monuments: in the last twenty years many of the most exciting modern buildings in London have gone up along its banks, including the Thames Barrier, the Millennium Dome and Canary Wharf.

As I have explored the Thames I have been struck by how the river changes character from one district to another. I travelled from the industrial Docklands in the east, now transformed into a mixture of new housing and high-rise office blocks, to the commercial and administrative centre in the City and Westminster. Beyond Chelsea the river becomes more residential, with clusters of houseboats at Battersea Bridge and Hammersmith. Putney sees the start of rowing

Houseboats at Chelsea (above).

An autumnal evening view of the Royal Botanic Gardens at Kew (right), with Syon Park on the left.

on the river, as the embankments give way to slipways for rowing clubs to launch their racing boats; and there are usually a number of oarsmen and women on the water between Putney and Kew Gardens. Their slender boats are vulnerable to the wash from a powered boat, so careful manoeuvring is needed to avoid a tirade of nautical abuse. At Kew the river becomes rural, with trees overhanging both banks as Kew Gardens and Syon Park face each other across the water. The journey to Hampton Court involves going through locks at Richmond and Teddington, as the Thames changes from maritime and tidal to an inland freshwater river.

I started off with a small sailing boat, equipped with a four horsepower outboard motor. Sailing turned out to be impractical, as there is restricted headroom under the bridges at high water, and I soon discovered that my engine was seriously under-powered when I was going against the tide. It was easy enough getting from Chelsea to Greenwich on a falling tide, but a real struggle to get home again. So I switched to a more practical, if noisier, inflatable speedboat with an engine powerful enough to take me skimming across the water. I had learnt the first lesson about the Thames: this is a tidal river. The tides come and go twice a day; the highest tides produce a rise in water level of up to 6.5 metres (21 feet) and run at speeds of up to three knots. This can produce fierce currents as the water swirls around the piers of the bridges; at Blackfriars, where there are three bridges very close together, a fast running tide makes the water very choppy, with waves up to 0.5 metres (nearly 2 feet) high. My small boat sits very low in the water, and it is quite alarming to slide from

the crest of a wave down into a trough, with the wave threatening to break over the stern. To avoid being 'pooped' calls for careful throttle control. I always advise my passengers to wear gumboots, as a surprising amount of water ends up in the bottom of the boat.

These powerful tides offer an easy ride to shipping, both to and from the sea. The Romans appreciated this when they built their new city of Londinium within reach of the tides. By the fifth century, when they left, the Romans had built a walled city which is still the nucleus of the modern City of London. The development of London, first as the capital of the kingdom and later as the trading and political centre of the British Empire, owes a lot to the ease of navigation on the tidal Thames.

For nearly two millennia Londoners have depended on the river in their everyday life. They fished and washed in it, and drank its water; they have used it in industries such as brewing, butchery, tanning and cloth-making. The Thames was also the capital's main highway, and provided the easiest way to get through the city at a time when roads were dirty and dangerous. It is no accident that until the nineteenth century all London's royal palaces were on the river.

This ready access to the sea is not without its dangers. In the eighth and ninth centuries the Vikings repeatedly brought their longboats to attack London. In the seventeenth century sea-going ships brought plague-carrying rats to the City. And during the Blitz in the last war the bombers of the *Luftwaffe* used the thin ribbon of reflective water to guide them to their blacked-out target. Above all there is the constant threat of flooding: over the centuries the river

Two artists (left) take advantage of a fine day to set up their easels on the foreshore at Rotherhithe.

Paddling at Richmond Riverside (right).

has often burst its banks, causing widespread damage to low-lying areas. Today we rely on the Thames Barrier to protect us from a catastrophic flood.

In the last fifty years we seem to have turned our back on our great river. We may enjoy looking at it, or living beside it, but we do not make much use of it. The building of the embankments in the nineteenth century has made it inaccessible for much of its length. The Thames has become an obstacle to be crossed by bridges or tunnels, not a highway to travel along. However congested the roads become, there is still no river bus to escape the traffic jams. The closure of the docks and the coal-fired power stations means there is little commercial shipping. When Tower Bridge lifts to allow a tall ship through, the commodity being brought into the City nowadays is a boatload of tourists. And there is certainly plenty for tourists to admire, as I hope this book shows.

Perhaps the emphasis on the Thames during the Millennium celebrations will stimulate interest in the river. Thousands of revellers will line its banks as the new Millennium dawns, and there is a proposal to raise the Thames Barrier overnight, creating a temporary lagoon for a massive water-borne carnival complete with fireworks and floating barges.

I have had great fun over the three years I have been taking these photographs. I always feel a surge of exhilaration as I leave my mooring and set off on a river trip. I love the vast space of the Thames, with its uncluttered horizons and open skies, and the diversity of the buildings along its banks. I get a particular thrill from following tall ships as they go through Tower Bridge when it opens, and looking up at the raised roadway. I even welcome the attentions of the river police, who usually come alongside to check on what I'm doing; I have not needed their help yet, but it's reassuring to know they're there if I get into difficulties. I would certainly call them if my morbid fear of finding a dead body in the Thames were to come true, but luckily this hasn't happened. I have enjoyed finding out about London's watery history, and getting to know a little of how the river behaves. However, there is one mystery that I cannot solve. Why, on every trip, do I see coconuts bobbing up and down in the water? How do they get there? Who throws them in? Where do they come from? Perhaps they're there just because they float.

A replica of Captain Cook's *Endeavour* sails past Canary Wharf (above), reminding us of the great days of sail.

At low tide Gabriel's Wharf in Southwark has a sandy beach where children can go mudlarking (right). They are wisely wearing rubber gloves.

Contents

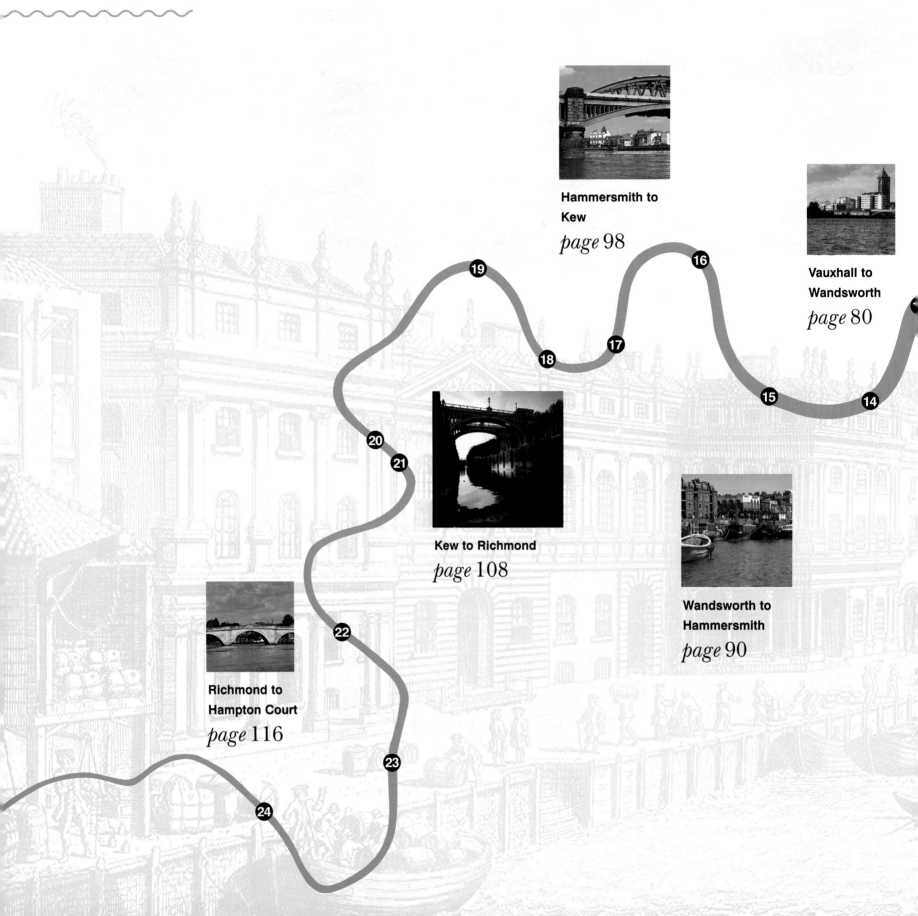

**Tower Bridge to
London Bridge**

page 40

**Blackfriars to
Westminster**

page 64

⑥ ⑤ ④ ③

⑦ ②

①

⑧

⑨

⑩

⑪

**London Bridge
to Blackfriars**

page 50

**Lower Pool to
Upper Pool**

page 32

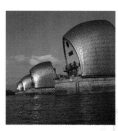

**Blackwall Reach to
Greenwich Reach**

page 10

**Westminster to
Vauxhall**

page 72

**Limehouse Reach to
Lower Pool**

page 20

Blackwall *Reach* to Greenwich *Reach*

Woolwich, Blackwall and Greenwich

In early 1953 300 people were killed when a disastrous flood swept through the East Coast of England. Canvey Island in the Thames estuary suffered the worst damage, as a combination of high tides and a storm in the North Sea raised water levels to unprecedented heights. Central London escaped on this occasion, but there had been bad floods in Westminster and Rotherhithe as recently as 1928. Until the building of the embankments in the 1870s, floods were a regular event in London. Westminster Hall, for instance, was inundated on several occasions during the sixteenth and seventeenth centuries, and in 1663 the diarist Samuel Pepys recorded 'all Whitehall having been drowned' after the 'greatest tide that ever was remembered in England'.

Today more than a million Londoners are at risk if another major flood leads to a serious breach of the embankments. The danger is increased by a general rise in water levels, caused by a number of factors. While London is gradually sinking onto its bed of clay, through the sheer weight of building, there are geological forces at work tilting Britain towards the south-east, at a rate of about 30 centimetres (1 foot) every century. Combined with rising ocean levels caused by melting polar ice caps, the result is a rise in the tides of about 60 centimetres (2 feet) per century.

The Thames Barrier was built at Woolwich to protect London from these dangers. The engineering firm of Rendel, Palmer and Tritton started work in 1975; seven years later it was complete. It is a huge construction, for at this point the river is 520 metres (over 1,700 feet) wide. Nine towers house the electro-hydraulic machinery for the barrier; covered in stainless steel plates, they suggest upturned hulls rising out of the water, or sails billowing in the wind. Between each tower is a steel gate: most of the time these lie flat on a sill on the river bed, allowing shipping to pass over. To lift the barrier, the machinery in the towers drives arms which rotate the gates through ninety degrees. This raises them 20 metres (66 feet) above the river bed to form a continuous dam to hold the water back. The useful life of the barrier will come to an end in 2030, when it is expected that sea levels will have risen to the point where it can no longer protect the capital.

The Thames Barrier Visitors Centre provides a good viewpoint for the latest engineering feat on the banks of the river, the spectacular Millennium Dome a couple of miles upriver. Designed by the Richard Rogers Partnership, the largest dome in the world occupies the site of a former gasworks. It has been built to provide the venue for *The Millennium Experience*, an exhibition divided into various zones, each celebrating a different aspect of the human spirit

The force of the tide is felt as far upriver as Richmond (right), and frequently catches out unwary motorists who park too near the river at low tide. At high tide their cars can be under a metre (several feet) of water.

The Thames Barrier, Woolwich (far right), was designed by Rendel, Palmer and Tritton, and built at Woolwich between 1975 and 1982 to protect the capital from the danger of flooding. At this point the river is 520 metres (over 1,700 feet) wide. By the year 2030 it is thought that rising water levels will make the barrier obsolete.

and man's achievements. The Dome owes its importance in the Millennium celebrations to its position two miles due north of the Royal Observatory at Greenwich, on the prime or 'Greenwich' meridian, at zero degrees longitude.

The earth's rotation on its axis from west to east means that there is no absolute position for calculating degrees of longitude. Lines of longitude are in constant motion, unlike lines of latitude, which have fixed points such as the poles and the equator. To provide universal map co-ordinates and to avoid confusion in international time-keeping, an arbitrary line of longitude is needed as a starting point for measurement. In 1884 an international conference in Washington DC agreed that the prime meridian should be at Greenwich, and that the 'Universal Day' should start on this line of longitude. This explains Greenwich's claim to be 'the place where time begins', hence its importance in the celebrations for the new Millennium, as the first second of 1 January 2000 will begin at the Greenwich meridian; although astronomers say that strictly speaking the Millennium doesn't really begin until 2001!

The Dome's technical details are as impressive as its appearance. Three hundred and twenty metres (1,050 feet) in diameter, the Dome is suspended from twelve yellow steel masts. Each mast is 100 metres (328 feet) long, and held in place by more than forty-three miles of high-strength cables. Forty thousand people can fit inside the Dome, which is higher than Nelson's Column, and large enough to cover Trafalgar Square twice over. The result looks like a cross between a modernist crown and a giant mushroom growing out

of the ground. On the western side of the Dome there is a circular opening for one of the ventilation shafts of the Blackwall Tunnel. The fabric of the Dome is translucent, lighting up the night sky over Greenwich with an eerie glow. Plans to build a cable car across the river from the Isle of Dogs came to nothing; this would have been a sensational way to get to the Dome. Instead, visitors can reach *The Millennium Experience* by Underground, but many will prefer to arrive by water; the approach from Greenwich Pier provides stunning views as you round the bend in the river.

Opposite the Dome, on the north bank, is another modernist building by the Richard Rogers Partnership: the Reuters Building of 1987–8. It bears the Rogers' hallmark of placing important, and usually internal, functions on the outside of the building: in this case, the staircase, visible on the left. This is the British headquarters of the international business and financial news organization Reuters. Subscribers to the service can obtain vital information on a vast range of subjects, from the gross domestic product of Brazil to a list of the world's airline crashes. The top storeys house a rooftop plant controlling the environment for the many computers; large satellite dishes reflect the nature of the business of the world's largest electronic publisher. Reuters moved here from Fleet Street in the late 1980s, following the trend among newspapers to forsake the old haunts for the brave new world, and lower costs, of Docklands. The exterior is clad in black glass which reflects the light of the evening sun back onto the water, discouraging prying eyes from seeing into the building.

Reuters Building, Blackwall (left). The world's largest electronic publishers moved their British headquarters to Docklands in 1988. The Richard Rogers Partnership designed the building, whose upper storeys are given over to computer cooling equipment and satellite dishes: a high-tech environment for a high-tech business.

The Millennium Dome at Greenwich (right). Designed by the Richard Rogers Partnership, the largest dome in the world has been built to provide the venue for *The Millennium Experience*. This photo was taken in early 1999, when the Dome was nearing completion. To get the mirror-like reflection in the water called for unusually still conditions: a combination of choosing a very calm day and waiting for the period of 'slack water' as the tide turned.

A little further along the north bank is another building closed to the public: the Isle of Dogs' Storm Water Pumping Station. Built to prevent the Isle of Dogs being flooded by a violent summer storm, this is one of the most exuberant modern buildings on the Thames. Designed by John Outram, and completed in 1988, it houses machines for pumping excess rainwater into the Thames. Basically a windowless shed, it was built to last for 100 years and designed to be proof against vandals and terrorists, and even earthquakes. Inside the building there is a complex series of pumps and ventilation equipment. Outside is complexity of a different sort. The architect has produced a building embodying a complicated allegory; in his own words, it is designed to 'imitate a river and a landscape, from which the storm-water flowed'. On the river front we see a pediment split in two by a ventilation turbine: the hole of the turbine represents a cave with a river flowing through it, flanked by the 'mountain peaks' of the split pediment. The big round half-columns below the Oriental capitals symbolize trees in a landscape, and the grey-blue bricks of the wall suggest a river cascading between them.

The next stretch of the river, between Woolwich Reach in the east and Blackwall Reach in the west, is fairly bleak except for a few quays, which usually have one or two large ships unloading. However, within a mile, going south past the Greenwich peninsula, is one of the great sights of London, the Royal Naval College. This occupies the site of the former royal palace of Placentia, beloved of the Tudors. Placentia was Henry VIII's birthplace and one of his favourite residences; from here he could easily visit the royal dockyards of Deptford and Woolwich, and inspect the ships being built for his navy. It was also the birthplace of his daughter, Elizabeth I, as commemorated by Samuel Johnson:

> On Thames's bank in silent thought we stood:
> Where Greenwich smiles upon the silver flood:
> Pleased with the seat which gave Eliza birth,
> We kneel and kiss the consecrated Earth.

Elizabeth's successor, James I, gave Greenwich to his Queen, Anne of Denmark, for whom Inigo Jones built the Queen's House in the early seventeenth century. Completed by 1637, after the Queen's death, the two-storeyed building closes the vista from the river. The Queen's House is a model of classical elegance, reflecting the influence of the architect's travels in Italy. With its simple proportions and lack of decoration, this Italian villa must have seemed strangely austere within the setting of the red brick Tudor palace. This simplicity is carried through to the interior: the main entrance on the river side leads into a hall whose proportions, 12 metres (40 feet)

in each dimension, are those of a perfect cube. After the Civil War, the remaining Tudor buildings were removed to make way for a new palace commissioned by Charles II from John Webb, a pupil of

Storm Water Pumping Station, Blackwall (above). Designed by John Outram and completed in 1988, this exuberant building houses machinery to pump excess storm rainwater into the Thames.

The Royal Naval College at Greenwich (right). The Queen's House (left), designed by Inigo Jones for Anne of Denmark, James I's Queen, is at the end of the vista.

Inigo Jones. The King Charles II Block, inscribed 'Carolus II Rex' below the pediment on the river front, is part of this scheme (the right-hand block as seen from the river). With its giant pilasters crowned by pediments and attic storeys, the effect is one of Baroque massiveness compared to the austere Palladian simplicity of the Queen's House.

When William and Mary came to the throne, they preferred Hampton Court to Greenwich. Greenwich's position to the east of London was subject to the smoke and pollution carried from the city by the prevailing westerly winds; this aggravated William's asthma. They decided to convert Greenwich into a hospital for seamen, on the model of the Royal Hospital in Chelsea (see page 83). In 1694 Sir Christopher Wren was asked to design the new complex. The twin domes crowning the central blocks are his great contribution. The west dome (on the right) is above the Painted Hall, with a grand ceiling painting by Sir James Thornhill, while the east dome is above the chapel. The colonnades, with their pairs of columns leading the eye towards the Queen's House, echo the pairs of pilasters on the King Charles II Block. The river front was completed by a block on the east to match the King Charles II Block. In the 1720s Defoe described Greenwich as 'compleatly agreeable by the accident of fine buildings, the continual passing of fleets ships up and down the most beautiful river in Europe; the best air, best prospect, and the best conversation in Europe'.

By the middle of the eighteenth century the hospital had more than 1,500 pensioners, but numbers declined, and in 1873 the Royal Navy took over the site to house the Royal Naval College, a training establishment for naval officers. After 125 years the college is moving out to make way for the newly founded University of Greenwich.

Charles II set up the Royal Observatory on the hill overlooking the hospital to resolve the longitude problem. This, the age of Isaac Newton and Edmond Halley, was a great period in English scientific achievement and astronomical discovery. In 1714 an enormous prize of £20,000 was offered by Parliament to anyone who could solve the greatest scientific challenge of the age. It was not until 1759 that John Harrison solved the problem with his famous series of clocks. He proposed a mechanical rather than a celestial solution: if a ship's navigator could keep accurate track of the passage of time while at sea, he could determine the ship's position east or west of Greenwich by calculating the difference in time between the two. Harrison was a Yorkshire carpenter and self-taught clock-maker, who had to overcome the scepticism of a scientific establishment reluctant to accept his revolutionary ideas. It was only the personal intervention of George III that secured him the prize, with the words 'By God, Harrison, I will see you righted'.

The Harrison clocks are among the treasures of the National Maritime Museum, which includes the Observatory Buildings, the Queen's House and Flamsteed House, designed by Wren for the first Astronomer Royal. Also at the National Maritime Museum is the Barge House, which displays the royal barge that William Kent built for Frederick, Prince of Wales, in 1732. With its gilded splendour and

Inigo Jones's pupil John Webb designed the King Charles II Block ('Carolus II Rex') of the Royal Naval College (left). In 1694 William III commissioned Christopher Wren to convert the Tudor royal palace of Placentia into a hospital for seamen. Beneath his twin domes (previous page) are the chapel and Painted Hall. The Royal Naval College took over the premises in 1873, but is soon to be replaced by the University of Greenwich.

lavish ornamentation, including mermaids and dolphins, this 'floating coach', as Kent called it, recalls the age of Handel's *Water Music*, a time when the river was the scene of much pageantry.

In permanent dry dock just to the west of the Royal Naval College is the *Cutty Sark*. Launched in Dumbarton in 1869, she takes her name from Robert Burns's poem *Tam O'Shanter*, in which a seductive young witch pursues the hero wearing a short skirt or 'cutty sark', which can also be seen on the ship's figurehead. In her day the *Cutty Sark* was one of the fastest clippers afloat, carrying tea from India and China: in 1871 she set a record for completing the voyage from China to London in 107 days. In many ways she was already an anachronism, as the age of steam was well advanced: Isambard Brunel's great steamships, the *Great Eastern* and the *Great Western*, had been launched more than ten years before. A shipping clerk, H. M. Tomlinson, records how, as a young man in the 1870s, he was told to send two consignments to Australia, which had to arrive two weeks apart. The first went on the *Cairnbulg*, a new steamship; the second on the *Cutty Sark*, which upset all his plans by arriving a month early, two weeks ahead of the *Cairnbulg*. Near the *Cutty Sark* is another, much smaller, exhibit, the *Gypsy Moth IV*: in 1966–7 Sir Francis Chichester sailed around the world single-handed in this little 16-metre (54-foot) yacht, at speeds equal to the average run of the *Cutty Sark*. The domed building to the right of the *Cutty Sark* is the entrance to a foot tunnel which replaced a ferry that had crossed the Thames at this point for over 200 years. The tunnel

was built at the end of the last century to provide dockers who lived on the south bank with an easy means of getting to work.

Looking up at the *Cutty Sark*'s three masts, and forests of spars shrouded with ten miles of rigging, we get a glimpse of the sort of view that was once so common on the Thames, but is now all too rare. Until the recent past, the Thames was crammed with shipping of all sorts, jostling for space on the busy waterway. In *Our Mutual Friend*, Dickens describes his hero as travelling 'in and out among vessels that seemed to have got ashore, and houses that seemed to have got afloat – among bowsprits staring into windows, and windows staring into ships'. Actually it's not clear who the hero of *Our Mutual Friend* is, unless it is the Thames itself, which provides the setting for so much of the action, and runs through the book from start to finish. Dickens' dark descriptions of the river, with its 'slime and ooze' peopled by the 'accumulated scum of humanity' are hard to recognize in the Thames of today. Thankfully the scene of the old man with his daughter eking out a living by robbing the pockets of corpses floating in the river which opens the novel would no longer be possible.

Henry Mayhew, in his account of *London Labour and the London Poor* lists over seventy-five places along the river where there were 'stairs', or stations, where travellers could hire watermen: 'Down the river, the Greenwich stairs are the most numerously stocked with boats.' Writing in the 1850s, he describes how most of the watermen's work was to take passengers to 'board any sailing vessels beating up for London', rather than to cross the river or to travel by water. One of the watermen he interviewed

The *Cutty Sark* (right) was one of the fastest clippers ever built, bringing tea from India and China. In 1871 she set a record for completing the voyage from China to London in 107 days. In permanent dry dock at Greenwich, she is now a museum commemorating the great age of sail. The domed building on the right is the entrance to the pedestrian tunnel linking Greenwich with the Isle of Dogs.

Gaffer Hexam looks for corpses in the Thames in the opening scene of *Our Mutual Friend* (far right).

described how in his own father's day 'a waterman's was a jolly life', but in the 1850s 'now we're starving. I've no children, thank the Lord for it: for I see many of the watermen's children run about without shoes or stockings.' The trade was being ruined by increasing numbers of steamers, which caused an alarming swell for the smaller boats. 'Last Friday a lady and a gentleman engaged me for two shillings to go to the Thames Tunnel, but a steamer passed, and the lady said, "Oh look what a surf! I don't like to venture;" and so she wouldn't, and I sat five hours after before I'd earned a farthing.'

To the east of the Royal Naval College is the 1837 Trafalgar Tavern, famous for its whitebait dinners, which featured in the wedding feast in *Our Mutual Friend*: 'What a dinner! Specimens of all the fishes that swim in the sea surely had swum their way to it'. A little further east again is Trinity Hospital, built in 1613 by the Earl of Northampton to house twenty male pensioners. Rebuilt in 1812, and resembling a toy castle with its Gothick castellated battlements, this charming row of almshouses is now dwarfed by the gaunt brick chimneys of the 1906 power station to the east.

During the Great Plague of 1665, many Londoners sought refuge from the disease on board boats moored in the river between Greenwich and Rotherhithe. Daniel Defoe, in his later account of the plague, tells how people had their provisions rowed out from the shore to avoid the infection, and imagines the scene from the top of Greenwich Hill: 'There must be several Hundreds of Sail, and I could not but applaud the Contrivance, for ten thousand People, and more, who attended ship Affairs were certainly sheltered here from the Violence of the Contagion, and liv'd very safe and very easy… As the richer Sort got into Ships, so the lower Rank got into Hoys, Smacks, Lighters and Fishing-boats; and many especially Watermen, lay in their Boats'.

Most of the interest in this stretch of the river is on the south bank, but on the north side, on the Isle of Dogs, facing the Royal Naval College, is the lively skyline of Dr Barraclough's Houses, designed in 1972 by Stout and Litchfield. With its steeply pitched roofs intersecting each other at acute angles, this group is all that survives of a housing scheme named after the local doctor. The project included over eighty flats, a pub and a community centre, but it fell victim to the oil crisis of the early 1970s. The rooms on the river enjoy some of the best views in London.

The Trafalgar Tavern at Greenwich (above) is one of the many historic pubs along the Thames. In Dickens's time it was famous for its whitebait dinners, which can still be enjoyed in its dining rooms overlooking the river.

Dr Barraclough's Houses (left) enjoy magnificent views of the Royal Naval College across the river from Blackwall. They are all that survives of an ambitious housing scheme, named after the local doctor. Designed by Stout and Litchfield in 1972, the project fell victim to the oil crisis of the early 1970s.

Trinity Hospital at Greenwich (right) was built in 1613 by the Earl of Northampton to house twenty male pensioners. This charming row of almshouses was rebuilt in 1813, and with its Gothick battlements resembles a toy castle.

Limehouse *Reach* to *Lower* Pool

The Isle of Dogs and the Docks

The meandering path of the Thames creates three peninsulas like interlocking pieces of a jigsaw: the Greenwich Peninsula on the south-east and the Rotherhithe peninsula on the south-west embrace the Isle of Dogs on the north. Originally known as Stepney Marsh, the name 'Isle of Dogs' has no satisfactory explanation: first recorded in the late sixteenth century, it might be a corruption of 'Isle of Ducks', or it might refer to royal kennels, or even to dead dogs washed up by the tide. Perhaps the name comes from 'Isle of Dykes': the few farms on the Isle of Dogs could only survive if the marshy land was drained regularly. In the seventeenth century the area looked like a scene from the Low Countries, with several windmills built on the western edge to pump the water out of the marshes – a memory preserved in the name Millwall. In the early nineteenth century, the largely uninhabited Isle of Dogs was identified as an area suitable for building the new docks which London so desperately needed. Trade on the river had reached levels of congestion and delay that had become intolerable.

Laws passed in the reign of Elizabeth I dictated that all goods arriving in London had to be unloaded at the 'legal quays', where customs duties were levied. These twenty quays, measuring just over 430 metres (1,410 feet), were all on the north bank between Old London Bridge and the Tower. In the eighteenth century an additional 1,000 metres (3,280 feet) of 'sufferance wharves' were created, where heavier and less valuable cargoes could be unloaded. Even so, these wharves were hopelessly inadequate for the volume of trade. During the eighteenth century, British overseas trade increased by leaps and bounds, and some three-quarters of all imports into Britain passed through the port of London. In 1705 1,335 ships arrived from foreign ports; in 1794 the figure had risen to 3,663. The total number of local vessels increased as well: in the Upper Pool there were mooring spaces for 545 ships, but more than three times that number were given permission to moor there. The quays could only receive the smaller boats; larger ships anchored in midstream, and had their cargoes transferred to 'lighters', barges which 'lightened' them of their loads. All this spelt delay for the ships waiting to unload – a delay which did not stop once they got their cargoes onto the quays. Perishable cargoes could sit on the quays for weeks, waiting for inspection by the customs officials. The warehouses provided at the legal quays had space for 32,000 hogsheads or large casks of sugar, but almost four times that amount arrived from the West Indies each year. The situation was made worse by the fact that most of it arrived in a short period during the late summer months, a time dictated by

William Hogarth's 1747 engraving (left) shows the 'Idle 'Prentice' being sent to sea to mend his ways; in the background are the windmills of Millwall and a man hanging from a gibbet.

One Canada Square, Isle of Dogs (right). This 244-metre (800-foot) high stainless steel skyscraper, by the American architect Cesar Pelli, is the centrepiece of the early 1990s development at Canary Wharf, intended to create a new international financial centre on land left empty by the closure of the docks. Canary Wharf takes its name from the banana trade with the Canary Islands.

the harvest and the prevailing winds. During the Napoleonic Wars, the need for ships to travel in convoy made the problem worse still.

There was systematic pilfering and theft from the ships waiting to unload, and the revenue officers were frequently corrupt. The situation was described in the 1790s by Patrick Colquhoun, a Scots-born magistrate who founded London's first police force, the Thames Police. In his *Treatise on the Commerce and Police of the River Thames*, he describes a situation where there was some £75 million worth of shipping on the river, 'all of it, more or less, subject to acts of peculation, fraud, embezzlement, pillage and depredation'. There was a whole vocabulary of river crime: 'scuffle hunters', 'night plunderers' and 'mudlarks' all specialized in different ways of carrying off large amounts of goods from the ships. Some of the worst were the 'river pirates' who would bribe or overpower the watch, set the ship adrift on the ebb tide and follow it to a 'convenient situation to be pillaged'. Colquhoun set up very strict rules for unloading cargoes: only the West India Company's own labour force of 'lumpers' were allowed on board ships being unloaded, and on 'quitting the Ship, every Lumper shall be searched by the Police Constable'. There were special rules to prevent the dockers hiding goods in their clothes: 'No Frocks, Trowsers, Jemmies, Pouches, or Bags, will be allowed'.

The West India merchants had long pressed for reform of the system, even threatening the City of London that unless something was done they would take their valuable trade elsewhere. One of their members, William Vaughan, advocated a series of inland docks,

modelled on Liverpool. The first to be built was the West India Docks, on the Isle of Dogs, to the designs of William Jessop. The inscription on the main gate reads: 'THE WEST INDIA DOCK IMPORT DOCK BEGUN 12TH JULY 1800 OPENED FOR BUSINESS 1ST SEPT 1802'. Colquhoun's and Vaughan's principles were incorporated into Jessop's layout of the dock, which was built behind high perimeter walls, and patrolled by its own police force. Within ten years the dock was handling about 500 ships a year, and the scale of theft and pilfering dropped dramatically. The West India Company calculated that within twenty years the docks had saved the West India merchants over £5 million.

In 1805 the Isle of Dogs became a genuine island when a canal was cut across the north to allow ships to bypass the bend in the river. In the first year almost 6,000 ships were pulled through the canal by teams of horses. But the success of the canal was short-lived, and by the 1830s it had been incorporated into the West India Docks. In the 1860s another dock was built on the southern part of the Isle of Dogs: Millwall Dock added a further thirty-six acres, and specialized in importing grain from the Baltic. In 1909 Millwall Dock was linked to the West India Dock, making one large system that covered much of the Isle of Dogs, with access to the Thames on both the west and the east. Early in the nineteenth century the old windmills of Millwall were removed to make way for John Scott Russell's shipyard, where Brunel built his *Great Eastern*. No larger ship would be built in Britain for almost forty years. The size of the ship and the position of the shipyard meant that she had to be launched sideways, a tricky procedure that nearly led to disaster

A fine Victorian warehouse in Limehouse in the process of being converted into flats; the lower floors are kitted out with balconies, while an attic extension provides space for Manhattan-style loft apartments, also with the obligatory balconies. On the lower floor two men in suits survey the scene, while builders are at work on the upper floors.

and caused the death of a workman. It took several attempts before she was successfully launched in 1859. The famous photograph of Brunel, standing in front of massive links of chain, was taken at the shipyard during her construction. A typical Docklands post-modern housing development, Ferguson's Wharf, has been built near the site of the shipyard.

The docks needed a labour force, and within fifty years the formerly uninhabited Isle of Dogs had a population of over 4,000. Within 100 years the population had reached 20,000, mostly dependent on work in the docks. The life of a London docker was one of poverty and uncertain employment, and from the beginning the dockers were prepared to withdraw their labour to ensure better conditions. In 1810 some 1,000 dockers went on strike, demanding a guinea a week, a seventeen per cent rise, but the strike was unsuccessful. Work in the docks depended on the number of ships arriving, which was always subject to seasonal variations, especially in the days of sail. It suited the employers to develop a system of casual labour, and the men were employed by the day or half-day. When business was really slack, there might only be an hour's work. The dockers would have to compete among themselves to be taken on for the work: 'call-on' was a scramble to be called by the foreman, as he selected those who would get work for the session. In due course the dockers organized themselves into a powerful trade union with fierce local loyalties, but their situation was harsh. In the 1880s one of the bosses, Colonel G. R. Birt, the general manager of Millwall Docks, wrote: 'the very costume in which they presented themselves ...

prevents them from doing work. The poor fellows are miserably clad, scarcely with a boot on their foot, in a most miserable state; and they cannot run, their boots would not permit them.' In 1889 the dockers successfully went on strike for 'the docker's tanner', or sixpence an hour. They gained the support of the better paid stevedores (whose job involved the more skilful task of loading, as opposed to merely unloading, the ships) and other port workers such as lightermen. The

Ferguson's Wharf, on the Isle of Dogs, is a typical Docklands post-modern housing development on the river, near the site of the shipyard where Brunel's *Great Eastern* steamship was built.

strike fund received £10,000 from the British public and the huge sum of some £24,000 from dockers in Australia.

The privately owned dock companies conceded most of the dockers' claims; and in so doing signed their own death warrant, for within ten years they were abolished and their functions taken over by the new Port of London Authority. The private companies had always followed a policy of fierce competition with each other, creating a downward spiral of dwindling profits. For the next sixty years the docks were a vital part of London's commercial life, and the dockers who worked in them developed a proud working-class community spirit. During the Second World War the docks were a prime target for the *Luftwaffe*, which inflicted severe damage in the Blitz. The worst attack came on Black Saturday, in September 1940. Four hundred enemy aircraft took part in the raid. They pounded the docks with incendiary bombs, which set fire to the timber stocks in the Surrey Docks, and 430 people died in the attack. After the war, in spite of the terrible damage caused by enemy bombs, the docks recovered their prosperity: in the 1950s the docks employed 30,000 men. But this was their swansong. The dismantling of the British Empire during the 1950s and '60s led to a halving of trade with the Commonwealth, as newly independent nations found it easier or more profitable to trade directly with America, Japan and Germany. The London docks, bedevilled by inadequate investment and frequent labour disputes, could not compete with the newly developed deep-water facilities at Hamburg, Rotterdam or Dunkirk.

Where the *Luftwaffe* failed, a simple metal box succeeded.

The shipping container, 2.4 metres (8 feet) high by 2.4 metres (8 feet wide) and up to 12 metres (40 feet) long, can be lifted straight from the hold of a large ship onto the back of a lorry, which can then be driven to a local distribution depot complete with customs facilities. Because the container protects its contents from the elements and petty theft, warehousing and transit sheds became redundant. Dockers needed about ten to fourteen days for 'stripping and stuffing' the average ship, whereas a container ship could be turned round in a couple of days. The world-wide trend to containerization finally put the London docks out of business. The dockers were faced with the destruction not just of their livelihoods, but of their whole way of life, indeed of their whole community. Between 1967 and 1981, one after another, the docks on the London Thames closed: the West India Docks and the Millwall Docks on the Isle of Dogs closed in 1980.

The following year the London Docklands Development Council, or LDDC, was established by the Conservative government of Margaret Thatcher, and given the task of regenerating the area. Docklands was designated an 'Enterprise Zone': planning restrictions were relaxed, and new businesses were enticed into the area with a favourable tax regime and exemption from paying rates for the first ten years. But the government was reluctant to pour public money into the area, preferring instead to attract private enterprise capital. In the words of its Chief Executive, 'the sheer scale of dereliction' facing the LDDC meant that 'the only way to tackle the problem without an enormous influx of public funds … was to generate a kind of critical momentum, a development snowball'. By the middle of the

Limehouse Waterfront. One of the few riverside residential terraces in Docklands is sandwiched between two pubs, The Grapes on the left and The House They Left Behind on the right. At low tide we can see how the houses are supported by piles driven into the shingle foreshore.

1980s the policy looked successful: £279 million of public funds produced a 'snowball' which pulled in five times that amount in private investment. Property developers were quick to seize the opportunities offered, and within a short space of time the Isle of Dogs became a huge building site.

At Canary Wharf the largest development was undertaken by the Canadian firm Olympia and York, at a cost of £4 billion. The overall plans were produced by the American firm Skidmore Owings and Merrill, one of the great names of American architecture, responsible over the years for many of the finest skyscrapers in New York and Chicago. Canary Wharf, with over twenty-six speculative office blocks providing space for 100,000 workers, looks more like a canyon on Wall Street than a traditional part of London's East End. It was conceived as a new financial centre, designed to replace the City of London. Its old buildings were considered inadequate for the new challenges of computerization and a growing number of financial businesses. By the mid-1990s Docklands had achieved enough prestige to attract the unwelcome attention of Irish terrorists: the 1996 Docklands bomb signalled the end of a ceasefire in the struggle over the future of Northern Ireland. The explosion killed two newsagents, and devastated one of the tower blocks at Sugar Quay.

Olympia and York commissioned the American architect Cesar Pelli to design a new landmark skyscraper, Cabot House, at One Canada Square. In Pelli's own words, it is a 'square prism with pyramidal top in the traditional form of the obelisk'. The tower stands 244 metres (800 feet) high. Clad in stainless steel to catch the light, it is visible from miles around. As you approach London from the south or east, its winking anti-collision light is usually the first sign that you are nearing the capital. The reflective exterior mirrors the mood of the day. In murky weather the tower shimmers gently and seems to disappear into the mist, while on a clear day the stainless steel blazes brightly with crisp sunlight, which is particularly effective from the river, as a swathe of light is reflected down onto the water.

As an individual building it certainly has style and presence, but the Canary Wharf development as a whole has more critics than friends in the architectural press: it has been condemned as 'a symbol of 1980s smash and grab culture', characterized by 'market-led opportunistic chaos' with 'a sprinkling of post-modern gimmicks'. The recession of the early 1990s led to a collapse in office rents, and by 1992 fifty per cent of the new office space in Docklands remained vacant. Olympia and York were losing £38 million a day. A few flagship companies, like the *Telegraph* group of newspapers, moved in, but not enough tenants could be found, and Olympia and York went bankrupt.

One of the main problems in attracting business to the area has been the poor public transport system. Instead of extending the London Underground to the Isle of Dogs, the Docklands Council preferred a cheaper overland scheme, the Docklands Light Railway (DLR). With a different gauge from the Underground and British Rail, the DLR cannot be properly integrated into the public transport system, making it inconvenient for many users. In recent years London's great natural highway, the Thames, has failed to provide a

Deptford Dockyards from a
Grand Panorama of London,
drawn by F. S. Sargent in 1844.

solution to the problem. The last privately run river bus service failed in 1993, for lack of proper integration with existing transport systems. In 1999 this is about to change as a new integrated transport policy for the capital is implemented, under the overall authority of London Transport. This is to include a new service on the Thames, operated by two ferry companies with a fleet of purpose-built boats. It will run from Westminster to Canary Wharf, stopping at several piers in between.

Besides the speculative office blocks, there are a number of housing schemes on the Isle of Dogs. The most striking is Cascades, built in 1988 to designs by Campbell, Zogolovitch, Wilkinson and Gough. High-rise public housing had a bad name by the 1970s, but this was different: a purpose-built luxury development of private housing for affluent young professionals working in the new Docklands. The whole project was built at breakneck speed and completed within eighteen months. The exterior has many nautical references: angular balconies jut out like the prow of a ship, and portholes pierce the wall below the sloping exterior emergency stairs. On either side of the stairs are terraces which 'cascade' down the building. The flats enjoy sensational views: those on the west face out across the river, while those at the back look across to Canary Wharf.

Since 1988 there have been many more housing developments on the Isle of Dogs. Typical of these is Dundee Wharf, built of traditional London brick shrouded by a lattice of balconies supported by pointed girders. Like Cascades, these developments tend to be aimed at prosperous professional tenants, rather than the

indigenous working-class East End community, for whom the changes in Docklands have brought few benefits. Some public housing schemes have been provided, but unemployment remains high among the families of former dockers. Social tensions are made worse by the high levels of immigration. In 1993 the Isle of Dogs elected the first British National Party councillor, who openly blamed Bangladeshi immigrants for the problems of the East End. The local football club, Millwall, enjoys a reputation for being supported by some of the tougher fans in the game. For the property developers this working-class community projects the wrong image of Docklands. Recently these conflicts have surfaced in the vexed question of fishing from the quays. The property companies see this as lowering the tone of their prestige developments, and are trying to ban the sport. The fishermen are resisting the change; when interviewed on television, one of them said: 'First they shoved us out of working in the docks, now they won't even let us fish there'.

The fact that it is worth quarrelling about fishing in the docks is a tribute to the water quality of the modern Thames. Although the building of the embankments and associated sewage works in the 1870s reduced sewage levels for a while, by the 1920s and '30s the quality of the water had deteriorated again, as a direct result of industrial pollution and increased amounts of sewage produced by the huge growth in London's population. Matters were made worse by bomb damage during the Second World War, so that by the 1950s eels were the only fish to be found in the river. Since then there have been major investments to improve the quality of the water. When

Dundee Wharf (left), another Docklands housing development of the late 1990s, stands near the entrance to Limehouse Ship Lock, which connects the Thames with the Regent's Canal.

Cascades (right) was built in 1988 to plans by Campbell, Zogolovitch, Wilkinson and Gough. This purpose-built luxury development on the Isle of Dogs was aimed at affluent young professionals working in the new industries in Docklands. There are many nautical references in the design: windows resemble portholes and balconies jut out like the prow of a ship.

oxygen levels in the river fall dangerously low, the Thames Bubbler steams up and down the river pumping oxygen into the water to allow the fish to breathe. Today there are about 100 species of fish in the London Thames, including dace, roach and flounder. Salmon are now thriving in the river, and are common enough for the Salmon Trust to build ladders to help them get past the locks and weirs on the Upper Thames. In 1988 more than 300 salmon were seen at Molesey Lock, near Hampton Court. At Cadogan Pier in Chelsea, where I keep my boat, small brown shrimps soon attach themselves to any ropes left trailing in the water, and there are enough fish to support flourishing populations of cormorants and herons along the Thames.

On the Surrey side of the river, going west from Greenwich is Deptford, built around the mouth of the Ravensbourne, one of the tributaries of the Thames. Old wharves are interspersed with modern housing developments. Historically Deptford was important as the birthplace of the Royal Navy, for it was here that Henry VIII set up the Royal Naval Dockyard. Close to the dockyard was Sayes Court, home of the diarist John Evelyn; in 1698 the Russian Emperor Peter the Great rented Evelyn's house while he visited the dockyard to learn about English boat-building. Evelyn had cause to regret his imperial guest, who left the house in a deplorable state.

To the west of the Isle of Dogs, back on the north side of the river is Limehouse. At Limehouse Basin a lock gate operates at high tide to allow shipping to go from the river to the Regent's Canal, which runs through East London and Islington, via Camden Town and Little Venice, to Paddington. At Paddington the Regent's Canal connects with the rest of the inland waterway network: you can go all the way to Birmingham on the Grand Union Canal.

The name Limehouse comes from the production of lime. Chalk was brought by river from Kent, and burnt in kilns here to make lime, an important building material. Unlike the Isle of Dogs, Limehouse was populated early on: by Elizabethan times there were over 2,000 inhabitants, mostly making their living from the river. John Stow, writing in the late sixteenth century, described Ratcliff Highway as 'a continuall street, or filthy straight passage, with Allayes of small tenements, or cottages ... inhabited by saylors and victualers'. Before 1600 most shipbuilding on the Thames had taken place further down the river, at Blackwall and Poplar; thereafter the increased trade with the Far East and Middle East created a demand for larger ships, many of which were built in shipyards in the riverside hamlets of Wapping, Shadwell and Limehouse, which grew steadily as a result. By 1700 the population of Limehouse had grown to 7,000, and this area was now considered part of London. In 1704 the new Tory government, in a gesture of piety, passed an Act for the Building of Fifty New Churches in London: St Anne's Limehouse is one of the handful actually built, to the designs of Nicholas Hawksmoor. From the river the exquisite white tower, capped by four pinnacled turrets and with the highest church clock in London, is clearly visible. Limehouse continued to be a prosperous centre of shipbuilding in the eighteenth century, and in the latter half of the nineteenth century Forrestts's yard was famous for supplying the Royal National Life Boat Institution with lifeboats.

St Anne's Limehouse (left) is one of Nicholas Hawksmoor's great London churches. In the reign of Queen Anne an Act of Parliament had proposed building fifty new churches, but only a handful were actually built. St Anne's (the name is a reference to the Queen, who had died in 1714) was completed in 1724. The distinctive white tower, capped by four turrets, was an important landmark for shipping on the river, and still has the highest church clock in London.

A view (right) of the Royal Naval Dockyard, Deptford, in 1797.

Dickens knew the area well. In *Our Mutual Friend* the Grapes public house was probably the model for 'The Six Jolly Fellowship Porters': 'a narrow lopsided wooden jumble of corpulent windows … with a crazy wooden verandah impended over the water'. Limehouse was home to London's first Chinatown, with 300 or so Chinese sailors and dock workers. They brought with them a reputation for gambling and opium dens: in Oscar Wilde's *Picture of Dorian Gray* the hero comes to Limehouse to smoke opium. In the 1950s London's first Chinese restaurants were established here, before Chinatown moved to Soho.

By the end of the nineteenth century Limehouse had become largely run down as the area become more industrialized, and many of its inhabitants found work in the West India Docks. London was primarily a port, and the life on shore offered the usual attractions designed to part sailors from their money: taverns, brothels and gaming houses. Pawnshops abounded for converting possessions into ready cash. Limehouse was one of the city's 'rookeries', a dense warren of streets into which the police rarely ventured. The notorious Ratcliff Highway, the haunt of prostitutes, cut-throats and gamblers, ran between Limehouse and the Tower, through Wapping and Shadwell. In 1811 it was the scene of the infamous Ratcliff Highway Murders, which claimed eleven victims within a few days. In 1872 the French journalist Jerrold toured the docks: 'Take Shadwell, Ratcliff Highway, Old Gravel Lane and Rotherhithe, and you find few differences … in the intensity of the squalid recklessness. By day and by night it is the same interminable scene of heedless, shiftless money-squandering of Jack ashore, in the company of his sweetheart.' The American Nathaniel Hawthorne was not impressed either: 'The shore is lined with the shabbiest, blackest and ugliest buildings that can be imagined, decayed warehouses with blind windows, and wharves that look ruinous … and the muddy tide of the Thames, reflecting nothing and holding a million of unclean secrets within its breast … is just the dismal stream to glide by such a city'.

The scene along the river front today is one of wharves and warehouses, but there is hardly any shipping and the disused warehouses are one by one being converted into flats. The ubiquitous metal balcony, the essential badge of a post-modern housing development, has sprouted out of many a warehouse loading door. Between the warehouses are the historic pubs: next to Shadwell Basin, to the west of Limehouse, is the Prospect of Whitby. Built in 1520, this is one of the oldest riverside pubs: frequented by smugglers and criminals, it was originally known as the Devil's Tavern. In the 1770s it took the name of *The Prospect*, a collier ship from Whitby moored in the Thames nearby. The Prospect of Whitby has many artistic and literary associations: Pepys, Dickens, Whistler and Turner all visited the pub.

An opium den in Limehouse (above), engraved by Gustav Doré in 1877.

The Prospect of Whitby, Wapping (right), is one of the oldest riverside pubs. Originally built in 1520, it was formerly known as the Devil's Tavern after its clientele of smugglers and criminals. In the 1770s it took the more respectable name of *The Prospect*, a collier ship from Whitby moored in the Thames nearby. Sitting in its riverside dining rooms at high tide you can almost believe you are afloat.

Lower Pool to Upper Pool

Wapping, Rotherhithe and East Bermondsey

To the west of Limehouse, on the north bank, is Wapping, scene of a bitter industrial dispute in the 1980s between News International, the publishers of *The Times*, and its print workers. The company was one of the first to leave Fleet Street, where the unions effectively controlled the production of the paper, and move to a new site with new technology. The old 'hot-metal' skills of the printers were made redundant by journalists working at computer terminals, and by electricians who looked after the new automated printing presses. The Thatcher government, happy to see the power of the unions broken, provided a huge police presence: there were many violent disturbances as the police struggled to protect the journalists and other workers from the printers blockading 'Fortress Wapping'.

News International's factory is on the site of the old London Docks, which had opened in 1805. For the first twenty-one years the London Docks had a lucrative monopoly: all ships carrying rice, tobacco, wine and brandy, unless they came from the West or East Indies, had to unload their cargoes here. Above ground the docks had the usual high perimeter walls, but below ground there was a vast network, covering about eighty acres, of brick-vaulted wine cellars, with an intricate system of ventilation. The vaults were dimly lit by

whale oil – gas was too dangerous in the presence of so much inflammable alcohol – and the whole scene was shrouded in a ghostly white fungus. This was a bonded warehouse, and much of the wine was stored in wooden casks. The cooper was a powerful figure as only he had the authority to remove and replace the bung in a cask. Prospective buyers were invited to inspect and sample the product 'in the wood'; wine merchants regularly brought their customers for tasting sessions, and by 1820 visits to the London Dock vaults had become highly fashionable. Virginia Woolf came in the 1930s: 'The wine vaults present a scene of extraordinary solemnity ... we peer about, in what seems to be a vast cathedral, at cask after cask lying in a dim sacerdotal atmosphere, gravely maturing, slowly ripening'. London Docks went the way of all the other docks, and closed in 1969.

Further along the river is another historic pub, the Town of Ramsgate. The infamous Judge Jeffreys, responsible for hanging some 300 supporters of the Monmouth Rebellion during the Bloody Assizes, was caught here in 1688. He had unwisely stopped for a drink while attempting to escape abroad by sea. He was taken off to the Tower of London and died shortly afterwards. To the left of the pub is the site of Execution Dock, where pirates and 'sea-rovers' were

Wine sampling at the London Docks (left).

Wapping Pier Head (right). These two terraces of elegant Georgian houses were built in 1811 for senior officials of the London Dock Company, on either side of a former entrance to the dock.

executed. After hanging, their bodies were tied in chains at the low-water mark, and left there until three high tides had washed over them. At nearby Wapping Pier Head are two rows of elegant Georgian houses built in 1811 for officials of the London Dock Company. Further to the left is the Victorian Gothic Oliver's Wharf. In 1972 this became one of the first Thames warehouses to be converted into housing; the large interior spaces provide luxurious accommodation. The old loading bays have been replaced by balconies with magnificent views of Tower Bridge.

In the mid-eighteenth century Wapping was a favourite haunt for the much feared press gangs: sailors coming ashore could be seized and forcibly 'pressed' into joining the navy. This fate befell Tobias Smollett's hero Roderick Random on Tower Hill: 'a squat tawny fellow, with a hanger by his side and a cudgel in his hand, came up to me , calling, "Yo, ho! Brother, you must come along with me." … after an obstinate engagement, in which I received a large wound on the head, and another on my left cheek, I was disarmed, taken prisoner, and carried on board a pressing tender; where after being pinioned like a malefactor, I was thrust down into the hold, among a parcel of miserable wretches'. The 'pressing tender' was a boat where the press gang's victims were kept until they were allocated to a ship in the navy. The life on board ship depicted by Smollett, himself a navy surgeon's mate in the 1740s, is one of extreme brutality and corruption. The sick bay was one of the worst horrors: 'Here I saw about fifty miserable distempered wretches, suspended in rows, so huddled one upon another, that not more than fourteen inches of

space was allotted for each with his bed and bedding; and deprived of the light of the day, as well as of fresh air; breathing nothing but a noisome atmosphere of the morbid steams exhaling from their own excrements and diseased bodies, devoured with vermin hatched in the filth that surrounded them, and destitute of every convenience necessary for people in that helpless condition.' With conditions like this it is not surprising that the navy was short of volunteers: more surprising is how effective the navy was as a fighting force, for this was the period when Britannia ruled the waves. The establishment of the British Empire in both the West and East Indies depended first and foremost on the strength of the navy.

Between Oliver's Wharf and Tower Bridge is the entrance to St Katharine's Dock, completed in 1828, to the designs of Thomas Telford and Philip Hardwick. Whereas the earlier docks had mostly been built on sparsely inhabited land, St Katharine's involved the forcible removal of more than 11,000 inhabitants and their houses, as well as the destruction of the ancient St Katharine's Church and its hospital. Many businesses, including a brewery, were also removed. Early conservationists mounted considerable opposition to the scheme in Parliament, but to no avail: the inhabitants were evicted, mostly without compensation. Modern left-wing historians see this as the urban equivalent of the rural practice of enclosure, whereby common land is expropriated for private profit. But in the event St Katharine's Dock was

Oliver's Wharf, Wapping (above), is a splendid example of an 1870s Victorian Gothic warehouse, converted into luxury flats by the architects Goddard Manton as long ago as 1972. Where there were once loading bays there are now balconies with sensational views of Tower Bridge and Butler's Wharf.

'Manning the Navy' (left), a press gang on Tower Hill in 1790, by Samuel Collings.

the least profitable of all the docks. As ships increased in size, the lock-gate at the entrance to the dock soon became too narrow, and in 1864 St Katharine's merged with the London Docks. After the closure of the docks in 1969, the dock basin became a marina. Ivory House, with its Romanesque clock tower, was converted into a mixture of apartments and offices above, and a range of shops at quay level. Other buildings were demolished to make way for the hideous Tower Hotel, surely the ugliest concrete monstrosity on the Thames.

To the north-west of Deptford, back on the Surrey side, is the peninsula of Rotherhithe. This is probably a Saxon name, meaning a harbour for either cattle or sailors. The earliest enclosed dock in London, the Howland Great Dock was built here in 1697. This was originally for fitting out ships rather than unloading cargoes, for the legal quay system was still in operation (see page 20). In the 1760s Howland was renamed Greenland Dock, after its connections with the whaling industry. In the 1800s this was incorporated into the Surrey Commercial Docks, the only enclosed docks on the south of the river. In their heyday the Surrey Docks also handled corn and the timber trade from Scandinavia. The 'deal porters' were famous for the huge loads of deal, or timber, they carried over their shoulders. A report from the 1920s concluded: 'to carry over a shaking slippery plankway a bundle of shaking slippery planks, when a fall would almost certainly mean serious injury, is work for specialists'. But the Surrey Docks suffered the same fate as those on the Isle of Dogs: the familiar problems of labour relations and dwindling trade led to their closure in 1970. Most of the docks were filled in, and the land used for new housing schemes. Two docks survived: South Dock became a marina, and Greenland Dock a watersports centre. Where once whaling ships unloaded their cargoes of whalebone and blubber, you can now learn to sail or windsurf surrounded by modern apartment blocks.

Following the curve of the Rotherhithe peninsula, past Cuckold's Point, we pass over the Rotherhithe Road Tunnel, built in 1904–8, with round brick ventilation shafts facing each other across the water. A little further on is the Thames Tunnel: the first underwater tunnel in the world took over twenty years to build, and was not complete until 1843. Tunnelling through soft soil is particularly difficult, as there is always a risk of the tunnel caving in.

St Katharine's Dock, Wapping (above), was completed in 1828 to the designs of Thomas Telford and Philip Hardwick. It was the last of the inner London docks to be built, and involved the forcible removal of more than 11,000 inhabitants, in spite of vehement protests in and out of Parliament. The docks, which were never a financial success, closed in 1969, to be replaced by a marina and shopping mall.

Howland Great Dock at Deptford (right) was the earliest enclosed dock in London.

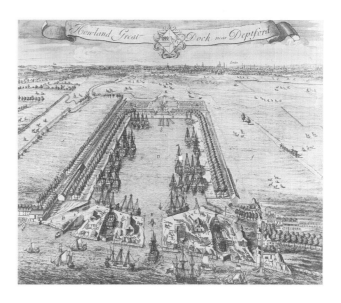

Marc Brunel, father of Isambard (who took over the work in 1827), devised a totally new system for building the tunnel. He got the idea from watching a wood-boring mollusc at work. The creature chewed its way through a piece of timber: it digested the wood as it ate, and extruded the pulp behind to line its tunnel. Brunel's system involved a tunnelling shield which divided the excavating face into small sections. Each section was excavated separately for 11 centimetres (4¼ inches) and then secured; when the entire face had been excavated in this way, the shield was inched forward, and the newly exposed area of tunnel lined with brick. This was a slow and painstaking process; many workmen died during the building of the tunnel, and the river broke through on five occasions. But the invention of the tunnelling shield was a major breakthrough, and the technique has since been used in many tunnels throughout the world. The Brunel Engine House in Rotherhithe has a display showing the machinery used in the construction. The tunnel soon became a popular tourist attraction, and several fairs complete with glass-blowing stalls were held under its brick arches, but after a while it became a disreputable haunt for prostitutes. In the 1860s it was taken over as a railway tunnel, and it still carries the London Underground from Rotherhithe to Wapping.

To the west of the Thames Tunnel is Princes Tower, at 93–97 Rotherhithe Street, one of the most successful modern blocks of flats on the river, completed in 1989 to the designs of Troughton McAslan. This seven-storey block has a tower jutting out towards the river, and the rounded living rooms with their tall windows enjoy 180-degree views over the water. The alternating bands of white concrete and dark windows give the feel of a 1930s lighthouse. Cantilevered balconies on the right project over the river, while on the roof there is a rounded glass observation tower like a ship's bridge.

To the west of Rotherhithe on the south bank is Bermondsey, covering the three miles of river to London Bridge. The name probably means 'Beornmund's Eye'; an 'eye' (or eyot or ait) is Old English for an island of higher ground among low-lying marshes. Originally the Thames was much wider and shallower at this point and, before it was built over, the south bank of the river was an area of islands barely rising above the water. Today Bermondsey is a varied area, which includes wharves and industrial warehouses in the east and the smart new development of London Bridge City in the west. The quaintly named Cherry Garden Pier in the east refers to a pleasure garden mentioned by Pepys. In the days before

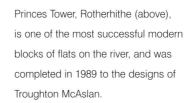

radio the pier marked the place where boats sounded their horn when they needed Tower Bridge to open.

In the 1770s this part of Bermondsey became a health spa, but by the next century it had become one of the most insalubrious slums in London. Bermondsey was the centre of the leather industry, and there

Princes Tower, Rotherhithe (above), is one of the most successful modern blocks of flats on the river, and was completed in 1989 to the designs of Troughton McAslan.

A fashionable couple walk their dog in the Thames Tunnel (left), completed in 1843.

China Wharf, Bermondsey (right), with its distinctive red façade is an exuberant 1988 design by Campbell, Zogolovitch, Wilkinson and Gough. On the ground floor the stern of a boat, *The Great Harry*, juts out over the water to form a balcony.

were many tanneries along the river. In Dickens's time the area just to the west of Cherry Garden Pier was known as Jacob's Island. In *Oliver Twist* the death of Bill Sikes takes place here, in 'the filthiest, the strangest, the most extraordinary of the many localities that are hidden in London' with its 'dirt-besmeared walls and decaying foundations; every repulsive lineament of poverty, every loathsome indication of filth, rot and garbage'. Things have improved since then, although there are still derelict warehouses with broken windows, rusty loading cranes, and decaying brickwork.

Bordering the area of Jacob's Island on the west is St Saviour's Dock; in the eleventh century this was used as a port by the monks of Bermondsey Abbey. At low tide the dock is mostly mud-flats, but at high tide it resembles a canal scene in Amsterdam. It is navigable for about half a mile, between tall warehouses now converted into flats. The footpath along the river crosses the dock entrance by means of an elegant bridge supported by a filigree of stainless steel wires: this swings out of the way to allow boats to pass through. To the west of St Saviour's Dock is the distinctive red landmark of China Wharf, one of the most exuberant buildings of the 1980s. It has been likened to a Chinese dragon, or a pagoda. Opinions of it vary: 'it's good stuff' says one critic, while another calls it a 'Post-Modern cartoon'. Half-moon windows punch holes out of the red concrete walls; on the ground floor the most whimsical of all the balconies on the river, the stern of a small boat, *The Great Harry*, juts out of the building. The design by Campbell,

Zogolovitch, Wilkinson and Gough was completed in 1988.

Next to China Wharf is the Design Museum, brainchild of entrepreneur, designer and restaurateur Sir Terence Conran. A disused 1950s warehouse was extensively converted to provide exhibition galleries for studying the history of the design of everyday objects, such as the telephone handset, the office chair and the vacuum cleaner. The museum is a temple of modernism, and the white stuccoed exterior continues the theme. The Blue Print Café, designed and owned by Conran, occupies the enclosed terrace on the first floor. On the museum's forecourt is a large head by Sir Eduardo Paolozzi. Other warehouses along Butler's Wharf are being converted into flats.

Continuing west we come to the Anchor Brewery at Horselydown, right next to Tower Bridge. John Courage bought a small brewhouse here in 1787; a century later a malt mill and boilerhouse were added. These were burnt down and largely rebuilt in the 1890s. The tall chimney at the eastern end served the huge boilerhouse; at the west end was the malt mill, topped by a pretty white cupola, with a walkway round the outside. A white clapboard look-out juts over the river front, above nautical looking portholes. Courage closed the brewery in 1983, and the whole block has been redeveloped to provide a mixture of flats and office space.

St Saviour's Dock, Bermondsey (above) was once the port for the eleventh-century Bermondsey Abbey.

The Anchor Brewery, Horselydown (left). There were once many breweries on the Thames in London. John Courage bought a small brewhouse here in 1787, but what we see today dates from the 1890s. The brewery closed in 1983 and has been converted into flats and offices by Pollard Thomas and Edwards.

The Design Museum, Bermondsey (right), housed in a converted 1950s warehouse, is the brainchild of Sir Terence Conran.

Tower *Bridge* to London *Bridge*

Upper Pool

A polar bear in chains, fishing in the River Thames at the Tower of London, was one of the sights of the city in 1252. A gift from the King of Norway, this was part of the menagerie which Henry III kept at the Tower. Until an elephant arrived, this time a gift from the French king, the bear was the star of the show. The Tower of London, originally built by William the Conqueror, has always been much more than a medieval castle: besides the royal menagerie (the famous ravens are descended from George IV's collection), it has also been home to the Royal Mint and Royal Observatory, and it still houses the Royal Armoury and the Crown Jewels. Throughout the Middle Ages and the Tudor period, the Tower served as a garrison and royal palace where the monarch held court, as well as a prison and place of execution. It has witnessed many violent events. Suspicious deaths include the Duke of Clarence, who drowned in a butt of malmsey wine, and the two princes murdered in the Bloody Tower. The executions of Anne Boleyn and Lady Jane Grey took place on Tower Green within its precincts, while less privileged victims, such as Sir Thomas More, were imprisoned in the Tower before being led to the public scaffold on nearby Tower Hill. In the First World War eleven spies were shot at the Tower, and in 1941 Hitler's deputy, Rudolf Hess, was briefly held here.

William the Conqueror's first building on the site was a wooden fortress, which he replaced by a stone building in 1078. St John's Chapel, part of the Norman keep, survives as a jewel of Norman architecture on the first floor of what is now the White Tower. The Tower is a large complex of buildings spanning the centuries. There are a number of half-timbered Tudor houses and offices; the Bloody Tower, Byward Tower, the moat and the royal apartments, as well as the four pretty cupolas clearly visible from the river, all date from the thirteenth and fourteenth centuries. There were two entrances through the outer walls: the one on the river has long been known as the Traitor's Gate, after the prisoners who were led through it on their way to execution. To add to their dejection, the falling tide caused the moat waters to rush out in a groaning cataract. The moat was drained in the 1840s; a recent proposal to flood the moat again would make the Tower look even more impressive.

The strategic position on a rising piece of land next to the river, and within the walls of Saxon London, was ideal for the Normans' purpose of consolidating their hold over the country, and intimidating the inhabitants of the city. The river provided easy access to the sea, which was important for the movement of troops and the supply of provisions to withstand a siege. It was also only a short

Watched by a large crowd, the Earl of Strafford was executed at Tower Hill in May 1641 (left).

The Tower of London (right) was originally built by William the Conqueror at the end of the eleventh century, but most of what we see today dates from the thirteenth and fourteenth centuries. Its riverside position provided water for the moat and meant that building stone and other supplies could arrive by ship. It also allowed prisoners to be brought in through the Traitor's Gate, no longer used but still clearly visible.

ENTRY TO THE TRAITORS' GATE

journey to the city of Westminster, where the Saxon kings had built a palace and abbey. Coronation processions from the Tower to the abbey could go by river in times of popular unrest: Richard III took this route.

Four centuries later a new river crossing was needed near the Tower. The Act of Parliament authorizing the new bridge decreed that the architectural style should be Gothic, and the exterior clad in stone, in deference to its ancient neighbour. Tower Bridge opened in 1894 and conceals a masterpiece of late Victorian engineering within its fantasy Gothic exterior. The two lifting sections of roadway, the twin towers capped with pinnacles and connected by a high-level footbridge, and the side spans with their curved lattice girders, all combine to create an outline that is instantly recognizable, and has become one of the symbols of London. If the appearance suggests an earlier age, the actual construction was ultra-modern. Like the early skyscrapers, the towers are built around steel frames to support the great weight, over 1,000 tons each, of the bascules, or see-saw mechanisms, which counterbalance the lifting roadway. The architect, Sir Horace Jones, described the towers as 'steel skeletons clothed in stone'. The original steam-driven hydraulic engines that raised the bridge lasted for more than eighty years until they were replaced by electric motors in 1976. The engineer in charge was Sir John Wolfe-Barry, whose father, Sir Charles Barry, designed the other great riverside symbol of London, the Houses of Parliament.

The decision to build a lifting bridge shows clearly the conflict of interest between river navigation and road traffic. In the late nineteenth century, as commercial activity increased to the east of London, encouraged by the development of the docks north and south of the river, road traffic became increasingly congested, and various schemes for new crossings were put forward. A few years before Tower Bridge was built, a proposal by Telford for a single-arch bridge at the site had been rejected because the lack of headroom would have restricted shipping. The authorities were very concerned that large ocean-going ships should not be discouraged from using the deep-water wharves at Billingsgate on the north bank and Hay's Wharf on the south, hence the insistence on a bridge that would open. The bridge has always given priority to river traffic: if a tall ship needs to come through the bridge, road users have to wait.

These days there are not many commercial ships visiting the quays and wharves, but in the busy summer months the bridge still lifts some fifty times a week. Typical movements needing a lift would be a large cruise liner or a visiting warship coming in to berth alongside HMS *Belfast*, or one of the handful of historically preserved London sailing barges visiting London Bridge Pier. Half a mile to the west, the restricted headroom of London Bridge prevents the passage of tall ships. The stretch of deep water between the two bridges is the last chance for a large ocean-going ship to manoeuvre and unload its cargo within easy reach of the warehouses of the City.

Under the shadow of Tower Bridge, at permanent moorings in the river, is HMS *Belfast*. Still in her camouflage colours, she is preserved here as a museum of life aboard ship in the Second World War, complete with a hammock for the ship's cat and a dental surgery

Tower Bridge opens (far left) to let a traditional Thames sailing barge through. When a new bridge was needed across the river in the 1890s, the conflicting needs of road and river traffic were met by providing a bridge that could open to allow large ships into the Upper Pool.

HMS *Belfast* (left), at permanent moorings opposite the Tower of London, is a floating museum of life aboard ship in the Second World War. Built in 1939, and still in her camouflage colours, the Royal Navy's largest-ever cruiser gives an idea of the size of the ships which can manoeuvre in the Upper Pool.

for sailors racked with toothache. Built in 1939, the *Belfast* is the only battle cruiser still afloat to have seen action on D-Day. At 11,000 tons the Royal Navy's largest-ever cruiser gives an idea of the size of the ships which could manoeuvre in the Upper Pool.

Sufficient depth of water for navigation was no less important to the Romans when they chose the site for their new city of Londinium. The area around London Bridge, besides being the furthest point inland with the necessary depth, had other advantages as well. The rising ground to the north would be safe from flooding and strategically easy to defend.

No less significant is the fact that it was still reached by the tides. At that time the river was much wider, and consequently slower, which in turn meant that the tides probably petered out before reaching the shallow waters around Battersea. The twice daily tides offer a free ride to shipping, even in adverse wind conditions. In the age of power-driven vessels it is easy to overlook the advantages of the tides, but to a primitive sailing vessel, unable to head into the wind effectively, or an oared galley dependent on human effort, they were of enormous benefit. The benefit would be felt particularly by a sailing ship negotiating the sharp turns around the Isle of Dogs. Any vessel moving up or down the river has only to wait for the tide to turn in its favour, and it will be carried before the tide for about six hours. If the journey can't be completed within that time, the ship can anchor or moor up to a quay and wait another six hours until the tide turns favourable again. Joseph Conrad, an experienced seaman, makes the point in the opening paragraph of the *Heart of Darkness*:

> *The Nellie, a cruising yawl, swung to her anchor without a flutter of the sails, and was at rest. The flood had made, the wind was nearly calm, and being bound down the river, the only thing for it was to come to and wait for the turn of the tide.*

London would neither have been built where it is, nor would it have been so successful, without its tidal river. A ballad, written to commemorate the opening of London Bridge in 1831, recognized this fact:

> *May Commerce set on every side*
> *With lofty sails displayed, sir,*
> *And on the bosom of the tide*
> *A brisk and rapid trade, sir.*

The Romans established a thriving port a little upriver from London Bridge, but it fell into ruins when they left, and it was not until the Saxon kingdom emerged in the seventh century that a settlement was re-established. By the late ninth century there was a Saxon market at Billingsgate, to the west of the Tower. Goods traded here included wool, coal, corn and especially fish, one of the essentials of life in medieval London. By the fourteenth century the Fishmongers' Company had established a monopoly in the London fish trade, which they carried on at Billingsgate Market. Although they lost this monopoly in 1698, they continued to control the bulk of the trade; under a charter granted by James I, 'fishmeters' appointed by the company still examine all fish passing through Billingsgate Market. The present building was designed in the 1870s by Sir Horace Jones, the architect of Tower Bridge. The long arcade along

This modernist blue glass block was built in 1985 for merchant bankers Midland Montague by Covell, Matthew and Wheatley.

the river front provided easy access to the market from the quays.

Billingsgate porters were famous both for their foul language and for the heavy loads they carried on their heads with the help of special leather helmets. When the market was transferred downriver to the Isle of Dogs in 1982, the old market building was converted into offices. But its fishy origins are proclaimed by the gilded dolphins on the corner towers and the fish on the weather vanes. To the east of Billingsgate is the Custom House; there have been custom houses on or near this site since the thirteenth century, including one designed by Christopher Wren after the Great Fire. The present Custom House was built in 1825 by Robert Smirke, the architect of the British Museum. From this building customs officers would patrol the Pool of London, and visiting ships' masters would queue up in the Long Room to declare their cargoes and obtain customs clearance.

To the west of Billingsgate is a blue glass office block. This aggressive but effective piece of modernism was built in 1985 for bankers Midland Montague by Covell, Matthew and Wheatley. On a sunny day, the river surface is enlivened by splashes of light reflected off its mirror-finish exterior. Still on the north bank, a little further to the west is Adelaide House, an office block built in 1926, a good example of the neo-Egyptian style of Art Deco popular after the discovery of the Tomb of Tutankhamun. For a while Adelaide House was the tallest office building in the city: it almost totally obscures the Wren tower of St Magnus the Martyr, which originally stood at the northern end of Old London Bridge, and its bulk prevents all but fleeting glimpses from the river of the 61-metre (202-foot) high fluted

column capped by a flaming urn. This is the Monument to the Fire of London, designed by Christopher Wren and Robert Hooke. In 1763 James Boswell wrote in his *London Journal* that he 'went up to the top of the Monument. This is a most amazing building. It is a pillar two hundred feet high. In the inside a turnpike stair runs up all the way … It was horrid to find myself so monstrous a way up in the air, so far above London and all its spires'.

The present London Bridge was built of pre-stressed concrete in the 1970s, replacing the elegant structure opened in 1831. John Rennie's London Bridge, which had succumbed to the scouring action of London's tides and become unstable, was sold to the United States, and re-erected across Lake Havasu in Arizona.

There had been earlier wooden bridges near this site. It seems likely that the Romans built the first bridge, probably with a drawbridge to allow shipping through. In 1014 a Saxon bridge was seized by the Danes, who were laying siege to London. The Saxon King Ethelred, with his Norwegian ally, King Olaf, burnt the bridge down to prevent further Danish attacks. After his death Olaf was canonized and the nearby church of St Olave was built in his honour. Other wooden bridges were built, but were destroyed by storm or fire, or simply fell down, as in the nursery rhyme. In 1176 a stone bridge was begun, and during its 600-year history it became one of the sights of Europe. Like the Ponte Vecchio in Florence, it soon became crowded with houses, shops and warehouses, some rising to seven storeys. In the middle of the bridge was a chapel to St Thomas Becket. The gatehouse on the southern approach, in Southwark, was used to

The Billingsgate Market building (left) has a long arcade to provide easy access from the quayside. The fish market closed in 1982, when it moved to Docklands, and the building was converted into offices by the Richard Rogers Partnership. The neo-Gothic Minster Court rises above the skyline.

The fishy origins of the Billingsgate Market building (right) are proclaimed by the gilded dolphins on the corner towers and the fish on the weather vanes.

Trading in full swing at Billingsgate Market (far right).

display the heads of traitors on spikes, after they were preserved by being boiled and dipped in tar. Many of those executed on Tower Hill, like Sir Thomas More, ended up here. The first head impaled in this macabre way was that of William Wallace, the Scots leader, in 1305. At the end of Queen Elizabeth's reign, in 1598, a visitor counted thirty heads on the bridge, 'as thick as pins in a milliner's cushion'. The grisly custom was finally stopped by Charles II, at the restoration of the monarchy after the Civil War.

Until the 1720s, when bridges were built at Westminster and Putney, Old London Bridge was the only bridge across the Thames in the capital. Foot passengers could pick up a small boat or wherry to ferry them across, and there was a notoriously unreliable ferry for horses and carts at Horseferry Road in Westminster (see page 75). The bridge suffered terrible traffic problems. In the eighteenth century special wardens were appointed, charged with keeping the traffic moving and preventing carts from stopping on the bridge.

The bases of the arches needed to be very solid to withstand the punishing action of the tides. As the bridge then had nineteen arches, the effect was to funnel the flow of water through these arches. On an ebb tide, when the water was flowing out, it poured through the arches in a terrifying cascade. Many boats attempting to 'shoot the bridge' came to grief, and cautious passengers would get out and walk round. Pepys records 'the passage of a Frenchman through London Bridge; where he saw the great fall, he begun to cross himself and say his prayers in the greatest fear in the world; and as soon as he was over, he swore *"Morbleu! c'est le plus grand plaisir du mond!"'*

The flow of water was used to drive mills which pumped water from the Thames to houses in the City. The first mill was set up in 1581 by Pieter Morice, a Dutchman, who proved its effectiveness by squirting a jet of water over the tower of St Magnus the Martyr. Mills revolutionized the supply of water in the City of London, and by the beginning of the nineteenth century watermills at the bridge were supplying some 18 million litres (4 million gallons) a day.

The arches also slowed down the flow of water above the bridge, acting like a weir. Besides making it easier for oarsmen to row against the tide, this also allowed the Thames to freeze over in a harsh winter. When the ice was solid enough to support the weight of stalls and booths, a 'frost fair' was held. One of the most famous was in the winter of 1683–4: the ice was hard enough to support horse-drawn carts, and a whole ox was roasted on the frozen river. One of the attractions was a hand printing press, which, according to John Evelyn, charged visitors six pence to print a souvenir card with their name on it. Charles II attended the fair, and his card survives in the Museum of London.

Until the 1960s, the Pool of London was alive with shipping visiting the wharves on both banks, but the whole system depended too much on manual labour and the city's days as a port were numbered. The same forces that led to the closure of the docks put paid to the wharves in the Pool of London. Dwindling trade, poor labour relations and containerization meant that business was lost to the specialized container terminals nearer the sea, in particular Tilbury and Felixstowe.

Adelaide House (right), by Sir John Burnet Tait and Partners, is a neo-Egyptian office block built in 1926. To the right, the tall fluted column capped by a flaming urn is the Monument to the Fire of London, by Christopher Wren and Robert Hooke. The Wren tower of St Magnus the Martyr can just be seen behind Adelaide House.

London Bridge (far right). There have been bridges on this site since the Roman occupation. The most famous was the medieval inhabited bridge (below), crowded with houses and shops. The nineteen arches acted like a weir, producing turbulent waterfalls as the tide went out. The present bridge is by Harold King and Sir Robert Bellinger (1968–72).

In the old days, ships would arrive at the wharves, and their cargo of imported foodstuffs, such as coffee, bananas or chilled New Zealand butter, would be unloaded one bag or crate at a time. Each sack or crate weighed no more than a docker could handle on his own, as he loaded it onto his hand truck before trundling it to the loading bay with its waiting lorries. Even with the advent of the mobile crane and the fork-lift truck, the system was inefficient, labour intensive and led to appalling traffic jams around Billingsgate on the north bank and Bermondsey on the south. It was also lively and picturesque, ensuring a bustle and constant hum of shipping activity within the Pool, and provided jobs for a large workforce close to the City. All this commercial activity gave the river a character and life which is sadly lacking today.

When the wharves of Bermondsey fell silent, there was a serious risk of the district falling into urban decay, as has happened further down the river at Greenwich. In the early 1980s, most of the river frontage between London Bridge and Tower Bridge on the south bank was acquired for redevelopment by the St Martin's Property Group. Their plan has combined new prestige office blocks, such as No 1 London Bridge, with careful preservation of older buildings, such as the headquarters of the Hay's Wharf company, originally founded on this site by Alexander Hay in 1651. Built in 1931 by H. S. Goodhart-Rendel, this very advanced building was supported on pillars that allowed easy access for lorries, while the ships were unloaded by cranes and derricks which were the last word in hydraulic and electrical machinery. The bold Art Deco lettering proclaiming the company's name and the decorative panels in gilded pottery on the façade were just as modern. The panels were the work of the sculptor Frank Dobson, and reflect the activities at Hay's Wharf: in a symbolic Chain of Distribution, bales, boxes, barrels and drums can be seen linking Capital, Labour and Commerce.

A few block to the east, the development at Hay's Galleria is remarkable for the glazed roof which snakes away from the river in an elegant curve, covering the former quayside of Hay's Dock. The river frontage has restored the original brickwork of Sir Thomas Cubitt's 1850s warehouse buildings, and the old dock has been filled in to provide a covered shopping arcade, one of the few spaces where the public can promenade under cover and gaze out across the river.

Between Hay's Galleria and Tower Bridge is an open space; in the year 2000 this will be redeveloped as the site for the headquarters of the recently established Greater London Authority. The new Mayor of London and his assembly will oversee London's transport, planning and corporate affairs, as well as having overall responsibility for the Metropolitan Police. The plans, which include a new jetty for the politicians to come and go by water, centre on a purpose-built 'giant bubble' directly opposite the Tower. The glass and stainless steel design by Sir Norman Foster has been compared to a huge disembodied car headlight, and opinions differ about allowing such militant modernism in this historic setting. Many will see it as a great building in the wrong place and regret that today's planners have not followed the example of the builders of Tower Bridge in their sensitivity to these ancient surroundings.

Hay's Galleria (left) covers the former quayside of Hay's Dock, built around a creek which once flowed into the Thames. In 1986 the old dock was filled in to provide a covered shopping arcade.

London Bridge City (far right). The area between London Bridge and Tower Bridge on the south bank used to bustle with activity as ships unloaded their cargoes before the closure of the docks and quays in the 1960s and '70s. The waterfront was saved in the early 1980s, when most of the district was acquired for redevelopment by the St Martin's Property Group.

Art Deco panels on the headquarters of the Hay's Wharf Company (above).

London *Bridge* to Blackfriars

The City and Southwark

Right next to London Bridge, conveniently close to Billingsgate Market, is Fishmongers' Hall, home of the Fishmongers' Company. The first Hall was burnt in the Fire of London, the second Hall of 1671 was demolished in 1827 to make way for the new London Bridge; the present building was built in the early 1830s, to the designs of Henry Roberts. It suffered serious bomb damage in the war, and has been carefully restored. The river front is very imposing. An arcaded basement projects forward, providing a balustraded terrace; above this rise six fluted Ionic columns supporting a plain pediment. The choice of the Ionic order for the capitals reveals Roberts as an architect of the Greek Revival School. The inside is equally grand, and contains several paintings of the Thames by Samuel Scott, whose work is an invaluable record of how the river looked in the late seventeenth century. Another treasure is the dagger reputedly used by Lord Mayor Walworth, a fishmonger, when he stabbed Wat Tyler to death at Smithfield in 1381. Tyler was the leader of the Peasants' Revolt, a rebellion against the unpopular poll tax. The fourteen-year-old Richard II confronted the rebels, and granted many of their demands. However, Tyler's disrespectful behaviour to the young king was too much for Sir William Walworth, who pulled Tyler from his horse and stabbed him.

The Fishmongers' Company is one of the City's ancient livery companies, so-called because they are entitled to wear distinctive clothes or 'livery'. In 1468 this was forbidden to most citizens by a statute of Edward IV in an attempt to suppress uniformed private armies. Each year the Lord Mayor and Sheriffs of the City of London are elected from the membership of the livery companies, and from 1422 to 1856 they went by barge from the City to Westminster to take their oaths of appointment. Since 1857 the processions have gone by road. The change was made inevitable by the increasing congestion and pollution in the river in the years immediately before the Great Stink (see page 64), and the increased flow of the river after the building of the embankments and the removal of Old London Bridge made control of the barges much more difficult. The final break came when the City lost control over the river in London to the newly created Thames Conservancy Board. Since 1883 the procession has gone to the Law Courts in the Strand, which had been completed the previous year.

The Lord Mayor's Procession or Show has always been a lavish event, and several livery companies maintained a ceremonial barge to take part in this and other pageants on the river. An account of 1575 describes the mayor going 'by water to Westminster in most

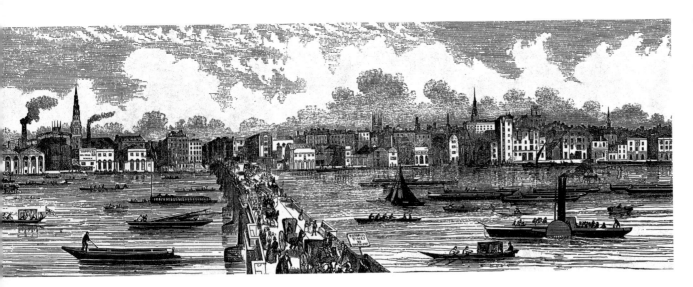

The original Blackfriars Bridge (left) built in 1760–9, from a *Grand Panorama of London*, drawn by F. S. Sargent in 1844. The present bridge was opened in 1869.

Fishmongers' Hall (right) is the home of the Worshipful Company of Fishmongers, who controlled the fish trade at Billingsgate for centuries, and still provide the inspectors at the new Billingsgate Market in Docklands. Their Hall was built by Henry Roberts in the 1830s in the Greek Revival style.

triumphant-like manner ... before him goeth the barge of the livery of his own company, decked with their own proper arms ... and so all the companies in order every one having their own proper barge ... and so passing along the Thames he landeth at Westminster'. The accounts of the Fishmongers' Company show that they paid £78 for their own barge in 1634. They have owned other barges over the years, and at Fishmongers' Hall there is a carved figure of St Peter, the patron saint of fishmongers, taken from an eighteenth-century barge. There are also Baroque angels blowing trumpets, and a scale model of the last barge built in 1773. Besides their splendid barge, the Fishmongers' Company regularly had a floating display at the Lord Mayor's Show with a model of a fishing boat laden with fish to be distributed to the poor. When the Lord Mayor's Show moved to the land, these exhibits continued to be called 'floats'.

Until 1857 the City of London was responsible for the Thames. The Lord Mayor was Admiral of the Port of London and entitled to be piped aboard vessels of the Royal Navy as if he were an Officer of the Flag. Regular inspections of the river were carried out on the City's behalf by a Water Bailiff, who used the *City Barge* for the purpose. The City owned at least three barges; one with eighteen oars was a very grand affair. The accounts for 1773 show that an upholsterer was paid almost £100, a huge sum at the time, for fitting up the barge with twenty-six crimson silk damask curtains, amongst other luxuries. In 1815 the Lord Mayor, Sir Matthew Wood, commissioned a new barge, which he named the *Maria Wood* after his daughter. At over 42 metres (140 feet) in length, the largest barge on

the river was too heavy to row and could only be manoeuvred with the tides. She took a prominent part in the grand opening of the new London Bridge by William IV in 1831. When these river processions stopped, the *Maria Wood* was sold, eventually becoming a pile-driver barge before she was broken up in 1920. Several of the livery companies sold their barges to Oxford colleges, who used them as headquarters at rowing regattas. Among the houseboats at Chelsea is the New College barge (see page 5), although this was purpose-built and did not come from a livery company.

In 1806 Nelson's funeral was one of the grandest processions ever seen on the river. The coffin was accompanied by some sixty vessels, including the barges of the Lord Mayor, the Fishmongers' Company and seven other livery companies, as it was carried from Greenwich to St Paul's Cathedral in Charles II's royal barge. Closer to our own time, when Sir Winston Churchill's body was carried along the river to lie in state at Westminster Hall in 1965, the cranes at Hay's Wharf dipped in unison as a mark of respect as the cortège passed under Tower Bridge.

The Queen still has a Royal Bargemaster who attends the sovereign on official duties on the Thames. When the royal palaces along the Thames were inhabited, there were frequent processions along the river from Greenwich to Whitehall and Hampton Court. One of the Royal Bargemaster's traditional functions, now carried out on land, is to transport the royal crown from Buckingham Palace to Westminster Abbey at the State Opening of Parliament.

A little to the left of the Fishmongers' Hall is Cannon Street

Cannon Street Railway Station was originally built in the 1860s as the terminus of the South Eastern Railway. The two distinctive brick towers, capped by leaded domes and spires, contained water tanks to power hydraulic lifts at the station. Cannon Street was rebuilt the 1960s.

Railway Station, originally built in the 1860s as the terminus of the South Eastern Railway. It occupies the site of the Steelyard, a former trading centre of the German Hanseatic League merchants. In the late Middle Ages they lived a life apart from other London merchants, even issuing their own currency and drinking exclusively Rhenish wine from stone bottles. Their privileges, always unpopular with London's native merchants, were revoked by Edward VI in 1551, and

the merchants themselves banished by Elizabeth I in 1598. Cannon Street Station was badly damaged in the Second World War. The two distinctive brick towers, capped by leaded domes and spires like latter-day Wren steeples, were retained when it was rebuilt in the 1960s. Containing water tanks to power hydraulic lifts at the station, these towers face out across the river. All the trains arriving at the station come from the south, across Cannon Street Railway Bridge. The bridge dates from the 1860s and is supported on groups of six stout cast-iron columns with delicate flutings; their Doric capitals were encased in concrete when the bridge was refurbished in the late 1970s.

Continuing upriver we come to Southwark Bridge. The present bridge of five spans was built between 1912 and 1921, replacing a bridge built 100 years before by John Rennie. The original bridge was famous for having a span of 72 metres (240 feet), the largest ever made of cast iron. For years Southwark was a toll bridge, whereas nearby Blackfriars and London Bridges were free – with the predictable result that they suffered terrible bottlenecks, while Southwark was hardly used. To spread the traffic more evenly, the City eventually bought Southwark Bridge in 1866.

Immediately to the left of the bridge, on the north bank, is Vintners' Hall. The Vintners' charter of 1364 gave them a lucrative monopoly on the wine trade with Gascony, at that time an English possession which included the famous vineyards of Bordeaux. Like the Fishmongers' Hall, the river front of the Vintners' Hall is a Greek Revival design, with fluted columns and Ionic capitals. Unlike the Fishmongers' Hall, however, most of what we see is modern, dating

Vintner's Hall (above) is the home of the Vintners' Company, who in 1364 were granted a lucrative monopoly on the wine trade with Bordeaux. Their Hall, with its 1820s Greek Revival river front, was rebuilt in the 1990s.

An engraving after Canaletto shows the City's skyline in 1747 (right), with Wren's City churches and St Paul's Cathedral framed by an arch of Westminster Bridge under construction.

from extensive rebuilding in the early 1990s. Each year the Vintners are involved in a quaint ceremony known as 'Swan Upping'. For centuries swans have been protected as royal property, but the Vintners, along with the Dyers, enjoy the privilege of owning some of the swans on the Thames. Every year the Royal Keeper of the Swans, assisted by swanherds from the Vintners' and Dyers' Companies, travels 'up' the river rounding up new cygnets and marking their beaks to show who owns them. The Queen's swans are left unmarked; there is one nick for the Dyers' swans, and two nicks for the Vintners'. The day's outing is rounded off with a riverside banquet at which swan meat is served. Swan Upping used to take place between Southwark Bridge and Pangbourne, but now starts higher up the river at Sudbury.

To the left of Vintners' Hall is Queenhithe. The name refers to Queen Matilda, Henry I's wife. In the early twelfth century she provided London with its first public lavatory, 'for the common use of the citizens'. In the Middle Ages there was an important harbour here, but the building of London Bridge restricted access to larger boats coming from the sea; the preferred dock was at Billingsgate. On the other hand, the same difficulty of going through the bridge meant that shipping coming from inland found it easier to dock at Queenhithe: much of London's grain supply came from the Upper Thames regions of Oxfordshire, Berkshire and Buckinghamshire, carried in ships docking at Queenhithe, 'the verie chiefe and principall water-gate of this citie'.

After passing a couple of modern office blocks, we come to St

Paul's Walk, a flight of steps leading up to St Paul's Cathedral. The views of Wren's great cathedral from the river are generally disappointing; the magnificent dome can be seen easily enough, but the lower storeys are everywhere obscured by buildings on the river front. Even St Paul's Walk provides only a fleeting glimpse of the south portico, with its pediment containing a carved phoenix and the word RESURGAM – 'I will rise again'. Wren's cathedral rose phoenix-like from the ashes of the medieval cathedral which was destroyed in the Great Fire of London. On 2 September 1665 the fire started in a bakery, and spread rapidly through the tightly packed wooden houses in the narrow streets. John Evelyn has left a vivid account of the blaze

which devoured, after an incredible manner, houses, furniture and every thing. Here we saw the Thames covered with goods floating, all the barges, and boats laden with what some had time and courage to save … Oh the miserable and calamitous spectacle! … All the sky was of a fiery aspect, like the top of a burning oven, and the light seen above forty miles round-about, for many nights … The noise and cracking and thunder of the impetuous flames, the shrieking of women and children, the hurry of people, the fall of towers, houses, and churches was like a hideous storm … London was, but it is no more.

Surprisingly only nine people died in the conflagration, but the fire devastated almost 400 acres within the city walls: forty-four livery companies, eighty-seven churches and more than 13,000 houses were lost. Wren and Evelyn both presented plans to the King for the complete remodelling of the City with straight roads and open

The Great Fire of London in 1666, viewed from Southwark (left).

Southwark Bridge (right) was built in 1912–21 to the designs of Sir Ernest George. The five-span steel structure replaced John Rennie's three-span bridge, built of cast iron in 1814–19. This view is to the east: through the arches Cannon Street Railway Bridge, London Bridge and Tower Bridge can be seen.

piazzas, along the rational lines of Louis XIV's Palace at Versailles, but these came to nothing and the City was rebuilt on its old medieval street plan.

The rebuilding of St Paul's Cathedral took many years, and was not complete until 1710, when Wren was almost eighty. The dome is a remarkable construction: a shallow interior dome is enclosed by a much taller exterior dome, with a height difference of 18 metres (60 feet). Between the two domes is a cone of brick supporting the weight of a lantern, topped by a gold cross. Energetic visitors who climb to the top of the dome can clearly see this construction, as the staircase runs next to the brick cone, between it and the outer dome. The overall height of the cathedral is 110 metres or 365 feet: perhaps the significance of the number 365 appealed to Wren, who was an Oxford Professor of Astronomy as well as the King's Surveyor-General. The two Baroque towers on the west façade were designed by Wren after the rest of the cathedral, perhaps as late as 1704. St Paul's suffered several direct hits from German incendiary bombs in 1940, but luckily escaped with minor damage.

Wren designed no less than fifty-two new churches to replace those lost in the Great Fire. These had to fit into the existing street plans, and display an astonishing variety and ingenuity in their designs. Most of the churches had steeples ranging in style from the Gothic of St Dunstan in the East to the Baroque exuberance of St Vedast-alias-Foster. St Bride's, Fleet Street, with its multi-tiered octagonal design, the prototype of many a wedding cake, is one of the most elegant; it is also one of the few visible from the river today. At the end of the eighteenth century the view from the Thames showed a London skyline which was almost entirely Wren's own work, with the spires of the City churches clustering round the cathedral. A number were lost in wartime bombing and others have been demolished to make way for new buildings; of the twenty-three surviving churches sadly few are visible from the Thames.

On the river front, to the left of St Paul's Steps, is the new red brick building of the City of London School for Boys, financed and governed by the Corporation of London. Between the school and Blackfriars Bridge is Puddle Dock, housing the Mermaid Theatre. Opened in 1959, this was the first new theatre in the City for 300 years. Unfortunately, the view from the river is all grim concrete. Castle Baynard once stood near here; Baynard had come over with William the Conqueror, and the castle was built to provide fortifications at the south-western corner of the City, matching the Tower at the south-eastern corner.

The two forts were connected by the city wall, which ran inland for two miles to enclose a roughly D-shaped area of some 300 acres. The Romans originally built the city wall in about AD 200. It was a massive construction, about 2.4 metres (8 feet) thick and 5.4 metres (18 feet) high, and punctuated by gates where the Roman roads left the city; these were later known as Ludgate, Aldgate, Cripplegate, Bishopsgate, Moorgate, Aldersgate, Newgate and Temple Bar. The outer faces of the wall were made of Kent ragstone, quarried at Maidstone and brought to London by boat: more than a million blocks were used. In the fourth century the military decline of Rome,

St Paul's Cathedral, by Sir Christopher Wren, completed in 1710. This cross section shows how the interior and exterior domes are separated by a cone of brick, which supports the weight of the lantern.

and the attacks by barbarian invaders on the town of Londinium, led to the building of a city wall along the river as well, totally enclosing the town. Although the wall fell into disrepair in the early Saxon period, large sections of it were later restored to provide the medieval city with its protective walls. By the eighteenth century, when London had expanded far beyond the old city, the wall was no longer needed and had largely disappeared.

By the second half of the third century, Roman London had taken over from Colchester as the largest city in Britain, as the population reached around 30,000. Excavations have revealed a pattern of villas built around courtyards, embellished with fine mosaic pavements. A house complete with its own bath-house and underfloor heating was found at a site in Lower Thames Street. There were many shops and warehouses, as well as large public buildings: a fort, bath-house, basilica, forum and an amphitheatre on the site of the present Guildhall. The basilica, which fulfilled the function of a town hall and court of justice, was the longest north of the Alps at over 150 metres (500 feet) long. A gold refiner's workshop has been unearthed, and another site contains the remains of a Roman fish-processing plant, producing the fish sauce known as garum from locally available species: herring, sprat and sand-eel. From the earliest habitation the Thames was therefore an important food resource, as well as a water supply. But above all it was a highway, as the prosperity of Roman London depended on trade carried on the Thames. There was an important port established in the first century near the site of the present London Bridge, which reached its maximum activity in the third century, with a lively import trade in Mediterranean wine and food, particularly olives and olive oil, as well as preserved fish and fish sauces. In the Museum of London we can see many artefacts imported during the Roman period: coins, lamps, pottery, glassware, silver jewellery, bronze brooches and carved figurines representing household gods.

This trade meant that there had to be a busy Roman port, but for years the precise position of the harbour was unknown. Paradoxically it was the final death of London as a port in the 1970s that led to the discovery of the exact location of the first London harbour. The large-scale building activity during the redevelopment of the City of London's waterfront led to the formation of an 'archaeological rescue unit', often working against the clock to preserve important finds before they were buried forever beneath modern office blocks. Archaeologists found traces of the original first-century Roman harbour, not on the present line of the Thames, but some 90 metres (100 yards) inland, to the north of modern Upper and Lower Thames Street. In the second and third centuries the river was progressively reclaimed; third-century quays have been unearthed on the site of the Custom House, part of a waterfront that extended for more than 450 metres (500 yards).

The Roman legions finally withdrew in 410, and by the end of the century Roman London seems to have been largely abandoned. Over the next centuries control changed hands frequently. The Saxon invaders set up kingdoms of their own, and a Saxon settlement grew up to the west of the Roman town, near the present Aldwych;

St Paul's Cathedral was built by Sir Christopher Wren after the Great Fire of London of 1666. Modern buildings along the waterfront prevent an overall view from the water; only the dome is clearly visible, and even that is usually hemmed in by cranes at work on new buildings in the City.

Aldwych means 'old wic' or old port. In 730 the Venerable Bede, writing in distant Northumbria, described London as 'the mart of many nations, resorting to it by land and sea', so this was an important community then, but in 851 a fleet of 350 Viking ships stormed London, driving the Saxons out, and the settlement was abandoned. In the 880s King Alfred the Great of Wessex mounted a counter-attack, and set up a fortified Saxon town, or burgh, inside the old Roman walled city in 886. From then on the City of London within its walls became the centre of settlement and commercial activity, a position it held unchallenged for centuries. When the Normans arrived in 1066 they incorporated the Roman walls into their fortifications at the Tower and Baynard's Castle.

In the thirteenth century the site of Baynard's Castle was given to the Dominicans, known as Black Friars because they wore black mantles as part of their monastic costume; the castle was rebuilt a little to the east. From the early fifteenth century Castle Baynard was royal property: it was rebuilt by Henry VII in 1487, but destroyed in the Great Fire. The Black Friars enjoyed royal patronage, and built a large and prosperous monastery on their site to the west. Most of this was destroyed in 1538 with the dissolution of the monasteries, but the name survives: Blackfriars Bridge even has 'pulpits' over the piers, alluding to its monastic past. The bridge was opened by Queen Victoria in 1869. Just to the east is Blackfriars Railway Bridge: like Cannon Street, all the trains arriving at Blackfriars come across the water, so the station needs its own bridge. It is right next to another, disused, railway bridge of 1864, its Romanesque cast-iron piers

supporting nothing; plans are afoot to build a pedestrian covered walkway across them.

Blackfriars has witnessed a number of gruesome events. In June 1982 the body of Roberto Calvi, an Italian banker connected to the Papacy, was found hanging from the bridge. More recently, in 1989, more than fifty party-goers were drowned near Blackfriars when their pleasure boat, *The Marchioness*, was run down in the dark by the *Bowbell*, a heavy dredger. In the aftermath of the disaster, the Thames Barrier was raised to hold back the tides to allow rescue divers to recover bodies from the river – one of the few times the barrier has been raised for an extended period of time. This was not the first time that a conflict between pleasure boats and commercial traffic had cost lives. Over a century earlier there was an even greater tragedy at Gallion's Reach, eleven miles below London Bridge. In 1878 the *Princess Alice*, a pleasure steamer returning from Sheerness to London Bridge, was struck by a collier ship, the *Bywell Castle*. Six hundred and forty day trippers perished; their bodies washed up on the banks of the river for several weeks.

Blackfriars also marks the site where the River Fleet used to join the Thames: the tributary ran a little to the west of the city walls. This was once an important harbour; in the twelfth century it was used for unloading stones for the building of old St Paul's. As the population increased during the Middle Ages, the Fleet became increasingly blocked with refuse and sewage, not helped by butchers using it to clean out the entrails of carcasses. It was dredged more than once, and in the 1670s was widened into a canal which took

The piers of Blackfriars Bridge (left) support 'pulpits' at road level, reflecting the religious origins of this area; the Black Friars, or Dominicans, had a large monastery on the north bank between 1221 and 1538, when it was 'dissolved' by Henry VIII during the Reformation. The bridge was designed by Joseph Cubitt and H. Carr.

Castle Baynard (right) was built by the Normans to provide fortifications at the south-western corner of the City, matching the Tower at the south-eastern corner. This engraving of 1790 is by A. Birrell.

barges as far inland as Holborn. It remained 'a stinking ditch', however, and things were particularly bad after a heavy shower, as described by Swift:

> *Sweepings from Butchers' Stalls, Dung, Guts and Blood*
> *Drown'd Puppies, stinking Sprats, all drench'd in Mud,*
> *Dead Cats and Turnip-Tops come tumbling down the Flood.*

In 1766 the attempt to keep the Fleet open was abandoned when the river was driven underground and covered over. Today Farringdon Road runs down to Blackfriars Bridge above the enclosed river. Nowadays the Fleet is used as a sewer and there is nothing to be seen: along with the Walbrook and the Tyburn it is one of London's 'lost rivers'.

Blackfriars Bridge leads to Southwark on the south bank: the district originally extended to London Bridge in the east. Today the Borough of Southwark includes Bermondsey and Rotherhithe on the river, as well as Camberwell and Peckham inland. The name probably comes from the South Work, referring to the southern approaches of London Bridge. When the Romans arrived in AD 43, most of the area south of the river was swampy and low lying; but at Southwark the ground rises slightly to provide a bridgehead. For centuries Southwark was the main approach to London from the south, with two Roman roads, Watling Street (now Old Kent Road) and Stane Street, converging on Borough High Street. All this traffic meant that Southwark became famous for its coaching inns and the breweries they supported. Close to the southern end of London Bridge lies Southwark Cathedral. Until the end of the nineteenth

century this was the parish church of St Saviour and St Mary Overie ('over the water'). The present building is the earliest Gothic church in London, and dates from around 1220. It fell into disuse after the Reformation: while Shakespeare's plays were being performed at the nearby Globe Theatre, there were pigsties and a bakery in the choir. After the Restoration the fortunes of the church improved, and at the end of the seventeenth century the distinctive square tower with its four pinnacles was completed. In 1905 St Saviour's became the Cathedral for South London, to meet the spiritual needs of the population south of the river, which had increased dramatically during the nineteenth century.

In the Middle Ages St Saviour's was controlled by the Bishops of Winchester, who rented much of the land in Southwark; they had their London residence at nearby Winchester House. Much of Southwark belonged to the church, with several monastic houses which were free from City jurisdiction, trade regulations and taxation: they formed the 'liberties' of the Clink and Paris Gardens. These included the district around Bankside, the street running along the river. This was notorious for its 'stews' or brothels, the rents of which provided the Bishops of Winchester with a large income; the prostitutes were known as 'Winchester Geese'. The bishops even laid down rules for running the brothels: any woman taking money from a man had to 'ly still with him' throughout the night. The street names of fourteenth-century Southwark give us some idea of its character: Dirty Lane, Foul Lane, Sluts' Hole and Whore's Nest, as well as the euphemistically named Maiden Lane and Love Lane.

Southwark Cathedral (left) was originally the parish church of St Saviour and St Mary Overie ('over the water'). The present building dates from around 1220, and is the earliest Gothic church in London. The distinctive square tower with its four pinnacles was completed in the seventeenth century. In 1905 St Saviour's became the Cathedral for South London.

This reconstruction of Shakespeare's Globe Theatre (right) is the brainchild of the American actor Sam Wanamaker. It was opened in 1996, and has central London's first thatched roof since the Great Fire of 1666.

Southwark's disreputable reputation was not helped by the sanctuary which St Saviour's offered to criminals and debtors fleeing from justice in the City. Again, the Bishops of Winchester profited from this, as they charged rent to those claiming protection. There were also a number of prisons right next to the sanctuary, including the Clink and the Marshalsea, where Charles Dickens' father was locked up for debt.

A replica of *The Golden Hinde* is permanently moored near the cathedral. The original ship carried Sir Francis Drake on his circumnavigation of the globe in 1577–80. He had set out on a mission to plunder Spanish possessions in South America; his successful seizure of gold and silver bullion led to a vigorous pursuit by the Spanish. Rather than risk capture coming home across the Atlantic, he decided to continue westwards across the Pacific, a journey which took him to the East Indies and round the Cape of Good Hope. At one stage he ran aground; cargo and cannon were jettisoned to save the ship, but he kept the bullion. On his return he was knighted by Queen Elizabeth for his exploits. The replica, built in Devon in the 1970s, is a full-size reconstruction of the original. Before becoming a museum in 1996 she too sailed around the world, covering 140,000 miles.

Bankside was free of the City of London's strict laws relating to public entertainment, and became famous for its bear-baiting pit, as well as for theatres, such as the Rose and the Swan. In 1597 the Mayor and Aldermen appealed to the Privy Council to close the theatres: 'they are the ordinary places for vagrant persons, masterless men, thieves, horse-stealers, whore-mongers, cozeners, coney-catchers, contrivers of treason and other idle and dangerous persons to meet together.' But their appeal fell on deaf ears: the following year saw the building of the Globe Theatre, where many of Shakespeare's plays were performed. During the Civil War the Puritans achieved what the City had attempted, and destroyed the theatre. The modern replica is the brainchild of the American actor Sam Wanamaker, who devoted years to completing the project; regrettably he did not live to see the theatre open in 1996. Performances are given 'in the round', with a 'groundling' audience who stand at the mercy of the elements. They are also unprotected from the actors, who mingle amongst them. The architect, Theo Crosby, insisted on traditional Elizabethan building methods and materials: the internal carpentry is held together with wooden dowelling pegs, while the outer skin of

the theatre is a mixture of plaster and goat hair. The Globe has London's first thatched roof since the Great Fire of 1666, albeit with a special fire-retardant coating. To the west of the Globe is a cluster of seventeenth-century houses; Wren is said to have lived in one of these, known as Cardinal's Wharf, while supervising the building of St Paul's.

Bankside Power Station, with its distinctive single chimney, was designed by Sir Giles Gilbert Scott and completed in 1963. No longer used, it is being converted into an extension of the Tate Gallery. A Millennium Bridge is planned to link the gallery with St Paul's Walk: this pedestrian bridge will be central London's first new river crossing for over 100 years. Bankside was a coal-burning station, and with its closure ended a long history of coal being shipped to this part of London. The industrial expansion of London in the eighteenth and nineteenth centuries, as well as much domestic heating, depended on coal brought by sea from Newcastle. The quantities of coal shipped south were enormous. Mayhew, writing in 1861, estimated that there were some 2,700 ships involved in the trade, employing over 20,000 sailors. In *Our Mutual Friend* Dickens has Gaffer Hexam chide his daughter for her dislike of the river: "'How can you be so thankless to your best friend, Lizzie? The very fire that warmed you when you were a baby, was picked out of the river alongside the coal barges.'" Taxes on coal provided ready money on many occasions: the rebuilding of St Paul's and the other City churches was paid for out of a special coal tax. Collier ships, many built at Whitby in Yorkshire, were a familiar sight on the river. These were resilient ships, capable of long journeys: the *Endeavour*, in which Captain Cook sailed on his first voyage of discovery, was a converted Whitby collier. In times of war colliers and their crews could be 'pressed' into the service of the navy. They were also at the mercy of enemy action on the run down the East Coast: in the two world wars many colliers were lost to German submarines.

On the north bank, to the left of Blackfriars Bridge, is the Unilever Building of 1930–1, designed by J. Lomax-Simpson with sculptures by William Reid Dick. This is the London headquarters of Lever Brothers, makers of soap and detergent. The building, on a curving site, is typical of its period: with its grand classical colonnade and muscular horses, it is reminiscent of public buildings in Fascist Italy. The building occupies the former site of Bridewell Palace on the banks of the old Fleet River. Like St Bride's Church nearby, the name of the palace refers to a well dedicated to St Bride. It was built in 1515–20 for Henry VIII. His son, Edward VI, gave the palace to the City, whereupon it became a prison and hospital. It was the scene of

Bankside Power Station (above) is being converted into an extension of the Tate Gallery by architects Herzog and de Meuron. This picture was taken in 1997, before work began. A new Millennium Bridge, designed by Sir Norman Foster, is being built for pedestrians to reach it from the north bank. It will be central London's first new river crossing for over a century.

Bridewell Palace (right), built in 1515–20 for Henry VIII, once stood to the west of Blackfriars Bridge. This 1817 engraving shows Bridewell as it was in the late seventeenth century.

many public floggings, and boasted a ducking stool and stocks. In his *Dunciad*, written in 1728, Alexander Pope refers to both the floggings and the canine corpses that could often be seen floating in the river:

> *This labour past, by Bridewell all descend,*
> *(As morning pray'r and flagellation end)*
> *To where Fleet-ditch with disemboguing streams*
> *Rolls the large tribute of dead dogs to Thames.*
> *The King of Dykes! Than whom, no sluice of mud,*
> *With deeper sable blots the silver flood.*

Although the flogging of female prisoners was not abolished until 1791, Bridewell was actually more humane than many similar institutions: it retained a medical officer and provided straw for the prisoners' beds – luxuries unknown in other London prisons at that time. The inmates were transferred to Holloway in north London when the prison closed in 1855.

To its left is the former home of the City of London School for Boys: the steep roof crowned by a slender pinnacled lantern, together with the busy stone façade and corner towers, give this 1883 building the look of a town hall in the Low Countries. In 1991 the school moved to its new site on the other side of Blackfriars Bridge. Immediately to the left of the school is the red brick Sion College; the mock Tudor Gothic building with stone dressings by Arthur Blomfield was opened in 1886. The large south window lights the library: Sion College, dissolved in 1996, was a society of Anglican clergymen with a large collection of theological books.

Continuing westwards along the north bank, we come to the gardens of the Temple. Oscar Wilde described an autumnal scene here, at a time when London's two main sources of energy were hay and coal. In the days before the motor car, the capital depended heavily on horse-drawn transport, fuelled by hay arriving by river barge from the countryside; at the same time London was often shrouded in fog from coal-burning fires:

> *Big barges full of yellow hay*
> *Are moored against the shadowy wharf,*
> *And, like a yellow silken scarf,*
> *The thick fog hangs along the quay.*
>
> *The yellow leaves begin to fade*
> *And flutter from the Temple elms,*
> *And at my feet the pale green Thames*
> *Lies like a rod of rippled jade.*

Today this area is dominated by the legal profession, but in the twelfth century it was a monastic house belonging to the Knights Templar, who took their name from the Temple of Solomon in Jerusalem. A crusading order founded to protect pilgrims in the Holy Land, they built a church, known as the Temple, a short distance from the river. The Knights Templar were disbanded in the fourteenth century, and their property passed to another religious order, the Knights Hospitallers, who in turn leased the land to lawyers. At the Reformation Henry VIII seized the property, and in 1608 the lawyers acquired the freehold of the land from James I on condition that they maintained Temple Church and its services in perpetuity.

This group of buildings to the east of Blackfriars Bridge has the mock Tudor Sion College of 1886 on the left; the former home of the City of London School for Boys of 1883 in the middle; and the curving Unilever Building of 1930–1 on the right. This was on the site of the former Bridewell Palace, which in the early sixteenth century became a famous hospital and prison.

Blackfriars to Westminster

The Strand, the South Bank and Whitehall

The Temple is the western boundary of the City of London. On the waterfront is King's Reach Watergate, built by Sir Joseph Bazalgette as part of the Victoria Embankment. The building of the embankments in central London in the 1870s totally transformed the look of the river. Previously, except where quays had been built for shipping, the river had a foreshore, and this was covered and uncovered twice a day by the rising and falling tides. Beyond Hammersmith, where there are no embankments, it is possible to appreciate today what the Thames must once have looked like for most of its length (see page 102).

The embankments were necessary to deal with the pollution of the river, which had become, in effect, a huge open sewer. Ironically the problem was made much worse by local improvements in hygiene, such as the closure of local cesspits and the increasing popularity of the new water closets in the early years of the nineteenth century, which increased the amount of sewage getting into the Thames. The river received most of London's sewage completely untreated; likewise, most of London's drinking water was drawn untreated from the incredibly polluted river. In the 1840s a series of cholera epidemics which claimed thousands of lives led to the founding of the Metropolitan Board of Works in 1855. The Board's remit was to provide for 'the better management of the metropolis in respect of the sewerage and drainage' of London; formerly these had been the responsibility of local authorities, which had proved quite unequal to the task. To achieve their aims the Board, which had London-wide powers, was to construct 'a system of sewerage which should prevent all or any part of the sewage within the metropolis from passing into the Thames in or near the metropolis'.

As the tides rose and fell they left huge quantities of sewage and refuse festering on the foreshore. For a few years not much happened, but the final straw came with the 'Great Stink' of June 1858, which galvanized Members of Parliament into action. A heatwave produced such a smell that life in the new Gothic palace on the river became unbearable; business could only be conducted behind windows draped with sheets soaked in disinfectant, and every day tons of lime had to be dumped into the river. In 1855 Joseph Bazalgette had been appointed Chief Engineer to the new Board of Works; after the Great Stink he set about providing a drastic remedy. The Thames was to be embanked for several miles in central London. In places the new embankments were built 150 metres (500 feet) out into the river; this eliminated the foreshore, so refuse could not accumulate and fester, and the narrowing of the channel forced the

Microscopia (left), or 'Monster soup commonly called Thames water, being a correct representation of that precious stuff doled out to us!!!' In this cartoon of 1828, William Heath satirizes the appalling state of London's drinking water.

King's Reach Watergate (right) is part of the Victoria Embankment. The Great Stink of 1858, when sewage had festered on the foreshore during a heatwave, had convinced the government to build embankments in central London to improve the flow of the river and divert sewage away from the city.

water to flow faster, which helped to keep the river clean. Bazalgette, in effect, built a huge box where the foreshore had been. Below the roads the 'boxes' contain sewers running parallel to the river; part of a new network of 1,300 miles of sewers, they intercepted the old sewers which used to feed straight into the Thames. The new sewers carried the sewage to outfall works, or treatment stations, further out in the Thames estuary beyond the eastern limits of the metropolis. Once treated the sewage was discharged into the Thames on a falling tide, which helped carry it out to sea.

The building of the embankments took several years, and was largely complete by 1874. From the river we see a succession of solid granite parapets, with mooring rings attached to lions' heads set in the wall. At street level Bazalgette created new roads running along the river, lit by elegant lamps decorated with sea creatures; in places like Cheyne Walk in Chelsea new gardens were laid out. The embankments also house Circle and District Line tube trains running between Blackfriars and Parliament.

As we enter the City of Westminster we soon come to another former religious house closed down at the Reformation. During the reign of Edward VI, his uncle the Lord Protector Somerset took over the land of the Bishops of Worcester and Chester, and built Somerset House. By 1550 Somerset was in disgrace; his pro-Protestant religious policy, in particular his attempt to enforce an English language Prayer Book, led to rebellions in Cornwall and Norfolk. At his uncle's execution in 1552 the young king does not appear to have shown much remorse; he merely remarked in his diary: 'Today the Duke of

Somerset had his head cut off on Tower Hill'. In 1554 the property passed to the Crown. In the early seventeenth century Somerset House was the setting for many splendid masques organized by Ben Jonson and Inigo Jones for Anne of Denmark, wife of James I, and for a while it was known as Denmark House. Inigo Jones, who designed the Queen's House in Greenwich for Anne (see page 14), lived here; he died in his apartments in 1652. During the Civil War the building again became known as Somerset House, and continued to be used for ceremonial occasions: Oliver Cromwell lay in state here in 1658. At the Restoration the house passed back to the Crown, and saw the first performance of Italian opera in England. The present building, a grand design in the neo-classical style by Sir William Chambers, was built to provide space for the Navy Office. Chambers started work in 1775, but the whole was still incomplete at his death in 1796. Today a screen of trees along the embankment hides most of the building from the river, but in Chambers' day the water at high tide lapped the arcaded basement, and there were two watergates for easy access to boats on the river. The upper floors present a grand façade to the Thames, and the central block has an open loggia topped by a pediment; above this is a green copper dome, set on a drum decorated with swags. In the pediment is a neo-classical scene of a sea nymph brandishing a trident, reclining on a horse with a fish's tail – an appropriately marine scene for the Navy Office. For years Somerset House housed various other government offices, including the General Register of Births, Marriages and Deaths; this was the place where anybody could consult the published wills of the rich and

Somerset House, the masterpiece of Sir William Chambers, was built to provide space for the Navy Office, hence the decoration in the pediment – a sea nymph brandishes a trident, reclining on a horse with a fish's tail. Work started in 1775, and was still incomplete at Chambers' death in 1796. The Courtauld Institute Galleries moved here in 1990.

famous. In 1990 the Courtauld Institute Galleries, with its collection of Impressionist and Post-Impressionist paintings by Renoir and Cézanne, moved here.

On the south bank, opposite Sion College, is the Oxo Tower, designed in 1928 by A. W. Moore. The eye-catching arrangement of the windows spells out the product originally stored in the warehouse below and was apparently a device to defeat a ban on advertising on buildings. The recent conversion of the warehouse by Lifschutz Davidson is among the most successful mixed-use developments in London. On the eighth floor is a Harvey Nichols brasserie, one of the smartest restaurants in London; a low-cost housing co-operative occupies the middle floors, with retail spaces on the ground floor. The local Coin Street Community, using the slogan 'Homes Not Offices', fought a long battle to defeat a plan by developers to demolish the Oxo Tower and replace it with a high-rise hotel and office space. It is part of the Gabriel's Wharf redevelopment, one of the few projects to avoid encroaching on the river. A conscious decision was made to give land back to the Thames, creating a mini harbour with a sandy beach at low tide where schoolchildren can go mudlarking (see page 7).

The river now turns south as it goes under Waterloo Bridge: the present bridge was built between 1937 and 1942 to the designs of Sir Giles Gilbert Scott, the architect of London's two power stations on the Thames. It replaced an earlier bridge of 1817 by John Rennie, described by Antonio Canova as 'the noblest bridge in the world'. At the southern end of the bridge is the South Bank Arts Centre. In 1951 the Festival of Britain was held here to celebrate the end of wartime austerity. The Royal Festival Hall, designed by the London County Council's own architects, was built in the same year, although its river front was faced with Portland stone and remodelled in 1962–5. Other buildings added to the complex in the 1960s and '70s include the Hayward Gallery, Queen Elizabeth Hall and the Purcell Room, the National Film Theatre and the National Theatre.

On the north bank the junction between Waterloo Bridge and the Victoria Embankment is the site of the former Savoy Palace. This had been royal property, but it was leased by Henry III to the future Count of Savoy. In 1381 Wat Tyler's followers attacked and ransacked the palace, which then belonged to John of Gaunt. The rioters threw a chest onto the fire, thinking it was full of gold which would melt. It turned out to contain gunpowder which blew the roof off the Great Hall, in the process entombing several men who had broken into the cellar and were drinking the wine held there: they were left to starve. The ruins were rebuilt as a hospital by Henry VII in 1505. The site was finally cleared to provide access to Waterloo Bridge in 1816–20, and the name survives in the Savoy Hotel, built in the 1880s. It got off to a flying start: the first manager was César Ritz, and his chef was Auguste Escoffier. Their rich and famous guests enjoyed such dishes as Peach Melba, created especially for the Australian soprano Dame Nellie Melba. There are now gardens along the river front, providing the backdrop for Cleopatra's Needle.

This granite obelisk was quarried in Aswan in Upper Egypt, and shipped down the Nile to Heliopolis in about 1475 BC. In the Roman period it was moved to Alexandria, perhaps as a memorial to

The Oxo Tower (left) was designed in 1928 by A. W. Moore. The glazing bars on the windows spell out the product originally stored in the warehouse below. The conversion by Lifschutz Davidson includes a Harvey Nichols brasserie and low-cost housing co-operative.

The Royal Festival Hall (right) is the main concert hall of the South Bank Arts Centre. It was originally built in 1951 to designs by the London County Council's own architects, Sir Robert Matthew and J. L. Martin. The river front was faced with Portland stone and remodelled in 1962–5 by Sir Hubert Bennett.

a son borne to Julius Caesar by Cleopatra. In any event her name is inscribed among the hieroglyphics. The obelisk is some 18 metres (60 feet) high, and weighs almost 200 tons: this was too much for the soft sand of Alexandria, where it toppled over. In 1819 the Turkish rulers of Egypt presented it to the British. The problems of transporting the obelisk to London were so great that the attempt was not made until the 1870s, and then it was nearly lost in a gale in the Bay of Biscay, in which several sailors drowned. Before it was erected on its present site a time capsule was buried in the foundations: besides razor blades, coins, bibles, newspapers and railway timetables, it contains photographs of a dozen of the most beautiful women of the day.

Behind Cleopatra's Needle is the equally monolithic Shell-Mex House, occupying an entire block on the Strand. This was originally the 800-bed Hotel Cecil, the largest hotel in Europe when it was built in the 1880s; in 1931 it was remodelled to provide the London headquarters for the Anglo-Dutch petroleum company, and given its distinctive Art Deco clock-face, which earned the nickname 'Big Benzine'.

In 1768 the Adam brothers, Robert and James, assisted by other members of the family, embarked on a large-scale speculative building development overlooking the river. They called their grand scheme the Adelphi (after the Greek word for brothers). It consisted of twenty-four terraced houses in typical Adam neo-classical style, built over a series of arched openings giving onto the river. They needed special permission to embank the river. This was vainly resisted by the City of London, and led Horace Walpole to remark:

'Scotchmen, by the name of Adams … have stole the very river from us'. Financially the Adam brothers were nearly ruined, and they had to be bailed out by a special lottery to raise the cash to complete the scheme. The Adelphi Terrace attracted a number of notable inhabitants: Robert and James Adam themselves lived here, as did the actor David Garrick. One of the more colourful characters was a quack doctor called James Graham. He ran a Temple of Health at the Adelphi, hung about with walking sticks, crutches and hearing aids discarded by his patients 'who being cured had no longer need of such assistance'. In 1781 Emma Lyon, the future Lady Hamilton who became Nelson's mistress, is supposed to have posed as the Goddess of Health at the Temple. For £100 hopeful couples could rent Graham's 'celestial bed', which offered relief from sterility. Chambers' Somerset House followed the Adams' basic plan of a large block built over an arcaded basement along the river front, and together they formed a splendid pair along this stretch of the Thames. However, government-owned Somerset House has fared better than the private, speculative Adelphi: when the Victoria Embankment was built in the 1860s, the terrace was cut off from the Thames; the central block, the Royal Terrace, was demolished to make way for a bland 1930s development also called Adelphi. The scheme is recalled in the names of John Adam and Adam Streets; and some original houses survive, although none can be seen from the river.

A little way beyond Cleopatra's Needle is Hungerford Bridge, or Charing Cross Bridge: another example of a railway bridge where the station is on the north bank, but the trains all come from across

Cleopatra's Needle on the Victoria Embankment (left).

Shell-Mex House with Big Benzine (right).

The Adelphi buildings on the Strand in about 1800 (far right).

the Thames. Charing Cross Station has recently been redeveloped by Terry Farrell to provide office space behind a large and impressive façade facing the Thames. In the 1840s Brunel built a suspension bridge at this point; when this was replaced by the present bridge in 1864 the chains were taken to Bristol to complete the Clifton Suspension Bridge. A footbridge runs next to the railway lines, providing easy access to the South Bank for art lovers going across the river. Through its piers can be seen the *Hispaniola* and the *Tattershall Castle*, two of the floating restaurants on the north bank. Beyond this is Whitehall Court, a large block with the lively skyline of a French Renaissance château, built in 1884 to house gentlemen's clubs.

The next mile or so is the heart of administrative London, from Whitehall to the Palace of Westminster. Henry VIII's Whitehall Palace, in his time the largest palace in Europe, used to stand on the river at this point: he died here in 1547. In the reign of James I grandiose schemes for rebuilding were drawn up by Inigo Jones, but only the Banqueting House was completed. Charles I amassed a splendid collection of paintings at Whitehall, but his associations with the Banqueting House were not so happy: in 1649 he was beheaded on a scaffold erected outside its balcony. Some fifty years later, when Whitehall Palace was destroyed by fire, only the Banqueting House survived. Now there are gardens along the river, and behind them various administrative buildings, including the Ministry of Defence.

Facing these across the river is Jubilee Gardens, laid out in 1977 to mark the Queen's Silver Jubilee. The Thames Path runs through this pleasant open space; in summer Jubilee Gardens is a popular venue for open air concerts, and throngs with office workers eating their lunchtime sandwiches. If they look down at the floor they can see that some of the paving stones are inscribed with poems celebrating the river; these 'pavement poems' include works by William Morris, Edmund Spenser and Spike Milligan. William Wordsworth's contribution is from his *Remembrance of Collins* of 1789:

> Glide gently, thus for ever glide,
> O Thames! that other bards may see
> As lovely visions by thy side
> As now, fair river, come to me.

I wonder if Wordsworth would have included among his 'lovely visions' the giant ferris wheel to be built near Jubilee Gardens in time for the Millennium. Eight hundred passengers will enjoy spectacular bird's-eye views of the Thames from the thirty-two 'gondolas'.

Along the river from the gardens is County Hall, the former home of the Greater London Council (GLC) before it was abolished by Margaret Thatcher in 1986, leaving London the largest city in the western world to have no representative government or strategic planning authority, a situation to be reversed in the year 2000 with the creation of a new Greater London Authority (see page 49). The premises have been taken over by an aquarium, a hotel and a hamburger bar. On the river County Hall presents a grand colonnaded crescent between two wings. It was built by the GLC's predecessor, the London County Council, between 1909 and 1922 to designs by the Edwardian architect Ralph Knott. The remains of a third-century Roman boat were found when the foundations were dug.

The Palace of Whitehall (left) in the late seventeenth century, with the Royal Barge in the foreground and the Banqueting House behind.

County Hall (right) was built as the headquarters of the London County Council, to designs by Ralph Knott (1909–22).

Westminster to Vauxhall

The Palace of Westminster, Pimlico and Vauxhall

Westminster Bridge, like most of London's bridges, is a replacement for an earlier one. The original was the first bridge in central London. Before it was built, if you wanted to cross the river you had to go round to London Bridge, or from the 1720s to the wooden bridge at Putney, or take the horse ferry at Lambeth or hire a boat. Pressure for a new bridge was at first resisted by City of London officials who feared the effect on navigation, by the Thames watermen who saw it as a threat to their livelihood and by the Archbishop of Canterbury who owned the horse ferry at Lambeth. But the expansion of Westminster in the eighteenth century made a new bridge essential. The watermen were bought off with £25,000 compensation and the Archbishop with £21,000. In 1738 Charles Labelye was given the task of building the bridge (see page 53), which opened in 1750. In 1802 the view of an early autumn sunrise from the bridge inspired Wordsworth to sing the praises of London:

> *Earth has not anything to show more fair:*
> *Dull would he be of soul who could pass by*
> *A sight so touching in its majesty …*
> *Ships, towers, domes, theatres, and temples lie*
> *Open unto the fields, and to the sky;*
> *All bright and glittering in the smokeless air.*

The bridge had fifteen arches, and between each arch was a recess covered with a little turret where people could shelter. James Boswell took advantage of this one evening in 1763, when he persuaded a prostitute to indulge him on the bridge, 'the whim of doing it there with the Thames rolling below us amused me much.' He doesn't tell us what the girl thought. The present bridge was built in 1854–62 by Thomas Page: for its day it had an exceptionally wide carriageway of 25 metres (84 feet) carried over seven arches of cast iron. The spandrels in the arches are decorated with coats of arms.

On the Albert Embankment, to the south of Westminster Bridge, is St Thomas's Hospital, which had been founded in Southwark in the early twelfth century and moved to Lambeth in the 1860s. Florence Nightingale was consulted on the design of the new hospital, and established her Training School of Nursing here. Formerly a disreputable occupation for illiterates and prostitutes, she transformed nursing into a respectable profession. The nurses were closely supervised by Florence Nightingale, and were expected to be neat, sober and orderly; nurses trained at St Thomas's are still known as Nightingales. The original buildings suffered severe wartime damage, and in the 1960s a new wing was built on the east of the site, close to Westminster Bridge.

This royal coat of arms (left) is on Westminster Bridge, built in 1854–62 by Thomas Page.

A view of St Thomas's Hospital (far left) in 1871, with Westminster Bridge in the foreground.

Throughout the Middle Ages the Palace of Westminster (right) was the main royal residence. When Henry VIII moved his court to Whitehall, Westminster became the administrative centre, and the home of the Houses of Parliament.

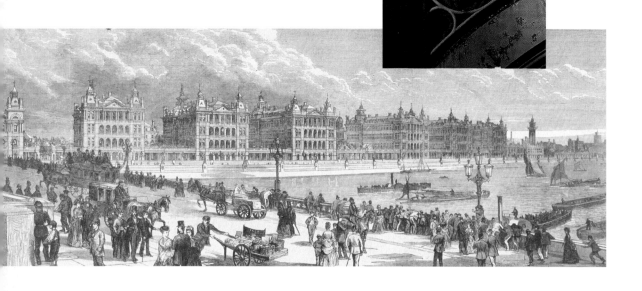

The Palace of Westminster is on the north bank. Formerly a royal residence, the palace now contains the Houses of Parliament. The development of Westminster as a royal stronghold, to the west of the City of London and away from its influence, dates back to the Saxon kings. Edward the Confessor lavished money on the Benedictine monastery of St Peter on Thorney Island, later moving his residence there and rebuilding the church known as the West Minster. Thorney was a marshy peninsula surrounded by drainage ditches and covered in 'thorny' brambles. Edward arranged for his mausoleum to be built inside his new abbey church, and it was here that William the Conqueror had himself crowned in 1066. Almost every monarch since has followed his example, and many have been buried here. As Francis Beaumont quipped in the early seventeenth century:

Think how many royal bones
sleep within these heaps of stones.

Most of Westminster Abbey as we know it dates from the twelfth and thirteenth centuries; however, the two west towers were the work of Nicholas Hawksmoor in the 1740s.

Throughout the Middle Ages the nearby Palace of Westminster was the main royal residence, until Henry VIII moved to Whitehall, leaving Westminster as an administrative centre and the meeting place for Parliament. It also housed the Court of Exchequer and, more fatefully, a huge accumulation of wooden tallies. These were notched sticks recording tax payments to the Exchequer. The sticks were split in two: one was given to the taxpayer as a receipt; the other was kept by the Exchequer. For proof of payment the sticks had to 'tally' when they were joined together again. When the Court was abolished in 1826, official secrecy decreed that all the Exchequer's tallies should be burnt in the furnace of the Lords' Chamber; in the process the chamber caught fire and by the next day the Palace of Westminster was a smouldering ruin. Dickens said: 'The sticks were housed at Westminster and it would naturally occur to any intelligent person that nothing could be easier than to allow them to be carried away for firewood by the miserable people who live in that neighbourhood. However, they never had been useful, and official routine required that they never should be, and so the order went forth that they should be privately and confidentially burned.'

The fire presented an opportunity to build a new palace, and a competition was held to choose a design 'in the Gothic or Elizabethan style'. Sir Charles Barry won the competition, and he turned to Augustus Welby Pugin for help with the Gothic decorative elements. Work started in 1837, and by 1852 both the House of Lords and the House of Commons were open. St Stephen's Tower, housing the famous Big Ben clock, was finished in 1858, and the taller Victoria Tower in 1860. The clock had a chequered history. The original specification was for the clock to be accurate to one second per hour, unprecedented for a clock of this size, with machinery exposed to the elements. Edmund Beckett Denison designed the mechanism, which exceeded the required accuracy. The bell, whose chimes have come to symbolize London, was originally cast in Stockton-on-Tees and transported down the North Sea and up the River Thames. The

bell-founders were unhappy with the unorthodox mixture of metals insisted on by Denison. In the event the sound was unsatisfactory, so Denison tried heavier and heavier clappers until a weight of thirteen hundredweight was reached, whereupon the bell cracked. It was broken up, melted down and recast by George Mears of the Whitechapel Bell Foundry. The recast bell, sounding the note E and weighing thirteen tons, was installed in the tower and became operational in May 1859. Within a few months the bell developed a crack; in spite of a stipulation from the foundry that the clapper was to have a maximum weight of four hundredweight, it transpired that Denison had installed one of seven hundredweight. The bell was modified to prevent the crack spreading, and a lighter clapper substituted, but the bell no longer sounds a perfect E. It's not clear why the clock came to be called Big Ben. Possibly the name refers to the corpulent Sir Benjamin Hall, the Chief Commissioner of Works responsible for the clock. The clock has remained remarkably accurate: in 1940 when a German air raid destroyed the House of Commons and the clock-face was badly broken, Big Ben lost less than two seconds.

The Palace of Westminster faces the river across a terrace where the members can entertain their guests: the Commons under the green awning, and the Lords under the red. Beyond the palace are the Victoria Tower Gardens, where there is a monument to Emmeline Pankhurst, the suffragette who was once locked up in the prison cell at the base of St Stephen's Tower. The stretch of river in front of the palace is the only restricted zone on the London Thames:

boats must keep to the far third of the river, near St Thomas's Hospital, as a precaution against terrorist attack.

The next bridge we come to is Lambeth Bridge. At its east end is Lambeth Palace, the London home of the Archbishop of Canterbury since the late twelfth century. The complex of buildings is centred around the hall of dark brick and stone buttresses, today largely hidden behind a screen of trees and the Albert Embankment. Inside there is a magnificent hammerbeam roof. There are plans to open the palace to visitors during the Millennium year. Directly opposite the palace on the north bank is Horseferry Road. Since the Middle Ages the archbishops enjoyed a monopoly operating the only London ferry allowed to carry horses and carriages. The ferry was a large flat raft; it was often unsatisfactory, as horses and carriages ran the risk of getting stuck in the mud at low tide when

they had to negotiate the exposed foreshore. Both King James I and Oliver Cromwell had narrow escapes when the ferry could not get to the shore, and there were frequent demands for a more permanent crossing. Lambeth Bridge was built in 1932, replacing a suspension bridge of 1862; it is the work of Sir George Humphreys and Sir Reginald Blomfield, who embellished the piers with charming dolphins.

The twin towers of Westminster Abbey (far left) can be seen behind the Palace of Westminster. The abbey was originally part of the Benedictine monastery of St Peter on Thorney Island, at that time a marshy peninsula covered in 'thorny' brambles. Edward the Confessor built a new abbey church and was the first of many monarchs to be buried here. Most of the exterior of Westminster Abbey dates from the twelfth and thirteenth centuries, except for the two west towers, which were completed by Nicholas Hawksmoor in the 1740s.

The embankments (above) were built by Joseph Balzalgette in the 1870s. Here, in front of Lambeth Palace, they are graced with elegant lamps with sea creatures entwined around their bases.

Lambeth Palace (left) has been the London home of the Archbishop of Canterbury since the late twelfth century. The complex of buildings is centred around the hall of dark brick and stone buttresses, today largely hidden behind a screen of trees and the Albert Embankment.

A succession of Edwardian blocks on the north bank leads to Millbank Tower, built in the 1960s by Ronald Ward and Partners for the Vickers Group. The thirty-two-storey tower rises above a podium at ground level. The tower's irregular ground plan creates glass walls alternating from convex to concave; as the curves catch the evening light, they cast reflections down into the water. The Labour Party recently moved its headquarters here.

A little further on is the Tate Gallery: opened in 1897, this was a gift to the nation from the sugar magnate Sir Henry Tate. The Tate houses two major collections: one of modern art; the other of British art based on J. M. W. Turner's bequest of a large number of his own paintings. The building was designed by Sidney R. J. Smith. Above a neo-classical portico a pediment is crowned by an imposing figure of Britannia, complete with trident, flanked by a lion and a unicorn. Behind her a glazed dome lights the entrance hall to the galleries. Most visitors are probably unaware that the Tate was built on the site of the former Millbank Penitentiary, or 'Tench', one of the most hated of the London prisons. In 1791 the philosopher Jeremy Bentham put forward new ideas of prison

management, and three years later he received a contract from the government to build a prison implementing his scheme. The prison was in the shape of a six-pointed star radiating from a central block; the layout allowed the officers in the central block to supervise the prisoners held in the six outbuildings. The riverside site was convenient for loading prisoners into ships, for many of the inmates were awaiting transportation overseas. The Tench covered seven acres of unhealthy marshy ground, and there were many outbreaks of scurvy and cholera before Bentham's ideas were discredited and the prison incorporated into the normal prison system in the 1840s. It was finally demolished in 1903 to make way for the Tate. On the embankment near the Tate is an abstract bronze statue of 1968: *Locking Pieces* by Henry Moore was a gift from the sculptor to the gallery. Given the prison history of the site, the title of the piece is all too apt.

On the opposite bank, next to Vauxhall Bridge, is 64 Vauxhall Cross. This is the world of James Bond and Spycatcher, for Vauxhall Cross is the new headquarters of MI6, the arm of the secret service concerned with threats from foreign countries and organizations. Their clandestine activities are carried out in a purpose-built block. To prevent eavesdropping, operatives apparently work in rooms surrounded by a 'Faraday cage' of wire mesh embedded in the concrete. The cage prevents unauthorized electro-magnetic waves entering or leaving the building. On the outside the building is far from anonymous: against a backdrop of dark green glass curtain walling there is a lively combination of ziggurats, spiky turrets and

The Tate Gallery (left) was a gift to the nation from the sugar magnate Sir Henry Tate. Designed by Sidney R. J. Smith, it opened in 1897 on the site of the former Millbank Penitentiary. This dismal prison, designed by the philosopher Jeremy Bentham, was built in the shape of a six-pointed star radiating from a central block.

Millbank Tower (above), now housing the headquarters of the Labour Party, was built in the 1960s by Ronald Ward and Partners for the Vickers Group. The thirty-two-storey tower's irregular ground plan creates curving glass walls that catch the evening light.

Locking Pieces by Henry Moore (right) is an abstract bronze of 1968, standing on the embankment close to the Tate Gallery. It is a gift to the nation by the artist.

projecting bays, all fashioned from pinkish concrete panels. The principal horizontal course is pointed up by fourteen conical trees, looking like so many Christmas trees. The design by Terry Farrell was completed in 1993.

Vauxhall Cross stands on land reclaimed from the river. Before the Albert Embankment was built the river extended to Goding Street, which runs behind the spy headquarters. Goding Street was formerly the river front of the pleasure gardens of Vauxhall, which started in Pepys' time. He describes a visit there in 1666 as 'pretty merry. Among other things, had a fellow that imitated all manner of birds and dogs and hogs with his voice, which was mighty pleasant. Stayed there till night.' In the next century, when an entrance charge was made to exclude the poor, Vauxhall became popular with the fashionable elite. The gardens were laid out in a series of avenues, with pretty pavilions and secluded arbours; public gardens like these offered the opportunity for a night out to respectable women, who were unable to visit clubs, coffee houses or taverns. Boswell remarked on Vauxhall's 'mixture of curious shew, – gay exhibition, – music, vocal and instrumental, not too refined for the general ear'.

In 1802 the craze for ballooning came to Vauxhall, when Mr Garnerin made an ascent. In 1837 Robert Cocking was killed when he attempted a parachute jump from a balloon. Dickens describes a balloon ascent from Vauxhall in *Sketches by Boz*: 'the balloons went up, and the aerial travellers stood up, and the crowd outside roared with delight, and the two gentlemen who had never ascended before tried

to wave their flags as if they were not nervous, but held on very fast all the while; and the balloons were wafted gently away ...' The pleasure gardens finally closed in 1859, but it is still possible to float above Vauxhall: an enterprising company keeps a tethered balloon ('Big Bob') on the site, and for £10 you can enjoy a ride up to 120 metres (400 feet) and enjoy sensational views of south London and the Thames.

The river, which has run north–south since leaving Waterloo Bridge, resumes its east–west course at Vauxhall Bridge. The first bridge on this site, built in 1816, was replaced by the present bridge in 1895–1906, designed by Sir Alexander Binnie. Five steel arches rest on granite piers decorated with statues depicting the arts and sciences by F. W. Pomeroy and Alfred Drury. A Pre-Raphaelite lady holding a model of St Paul's Cathedral represents Architecture. She

faces upriver towards Grosvenor Railway Bridge, serving Victoria Station: after about 180 metres (200 yards) on the north bank is a floating pontoon belonging to Westminster Boating Base, which keeps a flotilla of small sailing dinghies moored in the river. In the summer months their red sails are a frequent sight, as keen sailors practise their manoeuvres on this stretch of the Thames.

Vauxhall Bridge (above) was built in 1895–1906 by Sir Alexander Binnie. Five granite piers are decorated with statues depicting the arts and sciences by F. W. Pomeroy and Alfred Drury. A Pre-Raphaelite lady holding a model of St Paul's Cathedral represents Architecture.

64 Vauxhall Cross (right) is the new headquarters of MI6, the arm of the secret service concerned with foreign threats. The design by Terry Farrell was completed in 1993. Behind the building a tethered helium balloon flies from the site of the former Vauxhall Gardens.

This engraving of Vauxhall Gardens in 1751 by Samuel Wale (left) shows the Grand Walk at the entrance and the orchestra.

Vauxhall to Wandsworth

Chelsea and Battersea

The south bank is dominated by the distinctive fluted chimneys of Battersea Power Station, which unkind critics have likened to a giant upside-down table with its legs in the air. Today there are four chimneys standing 90 metres (300 feet) high, but when the station first opened in the mid-1930s there was only one at each end. The station was later doubled in size, and building was complete by 1953. The exterior designs were by Sir Giles Gilbert Scott, who originally proposed square chimneys, closer in plan to his other power station at Bankside (see page 62). Both were coal-fired stations, and their riverside sites were chosen to provide easy access to collier ships from the north-east bringing coal down the North Sea and up the Thames. Resembling sinister praying mantises waiting to strike, cranes for unloading the coal still stand on the river front at Battersea, but the station closed in 1983. Plans for converting the building into a leisure complex failed in the early 1990s when the developers ran out of money, and this great example of industrial architecture faces an uncertain future. Brave souls who want a bird's-eye view of the empty shell can go bungee-jumping from a 90-metre (300-foot) high crane at nearby 'Adrenalin Village'.

The next two river crossings are close together: within 180 metres (200 yards) of Grosvenor or Victoria Railway Bridge is Chelsea Bridge. When the original bridge at Chelsea was built in the 1850s, the excavations unearthed many human bones, as well as British and Roman weapons, so this must have been the site of an important battle. At that time it was probably possible to ford the river here, so the battle was presumably to gain control of the river crossing. The Romans would have been attacking from the south bank, or Battersea side, and legend has it that they only won the day when they brought an elephant into the fray. The present suspension bridge looks particularly fine when illuminated at night. It was designed in 1934 by Rendel, Palmer and Tritton; forty years later the same firm was responsible for the Thames Barrier at Woolwich (see page 10).

Chelsea has had a distinctive character since the days of Sir Thomas More, who built a house here in the 1520s. Chelsea was then a small village, separated from Westminster by open fields, but conveniently accessible by water. More kept a barge with eight watermen, but when he fell from favour with Henry VIII he had to give the barge away. Chelsea became known as the 'Village of

Coal arriving in barges at Battersea (left) was unloaded onto conveyor belts by these cranes with their 'grabber' buckets. Although Sir Giles Gilbert Scott's Battersea Power Station (right) has been closed since 1983, these cranes still stand like silent sentries on the quayside.

Chelsea Embankment (far left): this view taken from Battersea Bridge shows Cheyne Walk after the building of the embankments in the 1870s. Old Chelsea Bridge, built in the 1850s, is in the distance.

Palaces' when other figures of the Tudor period, including the Earl of Shrewsbury and the Duke of Norfolk, as well as Henry VIII himself, built country houses here; none of these Tudor palaces survive.

The earliest large building in Chelsea is the Royal Hospital, occupying grounds to the west of Chelsea Bridge. In 1682 Charles II commissioned Sir Christopher Wren to design a hospital where army veterans could be cared for, along the lines of Louis XIV's Hôtel des Invalides in Paris. Ten years later the building was finished, and remains substantially unchanged to this day. The design is simpler than the later Greenwich Hospital (see page 15); Wren himself described it as 'pleasantly seated on a plane of gravell overlooking the Meadowes and the River Thames, which lies to the South, and having a Pleasant view of the country on all sides. It consists of a large Courte built on three sides, the fourth side next to the Thames lying open to the gardens and Meadows.' The hospital is mostly built of red brick, relieved by touches of stone in the centrepieces of the three blocks. The central block has a colonnade; in the centre there is a plain Tuscan portico and pediment, with a domed lantern above. Wren planned formal gardens leading down to the Thames with two canals at right angles to the river, stocked with fish and water birds. Over time the canals became blocked with weeds and refuse, including the usual dead dogs, and had to be filled in. The Royal Hospital opened in 1689, before the buildings were finished, with space for 476 pensioners. Chelsea Pensioners in their traditional blue and scarlet uniforms are still a familiar sight in the streets of Chelsea, although they are no longer expected to perform military duties. In the early

days the inmates provided a patrol to protect citizens against street robbery, which was a frequent threat in the country lanes leading to the West End through modern Belgravia. For a few days in May the grounds of the hospital are taken over by the Chelsea Flower Show.

The first Paymaster General and Treasurer to the Royal Hospital was the Earl of Ranelagh, who used his position to expropriate almost a third of the hospital's land, and embezzled enough money from the hospital treasury to build himself a smart

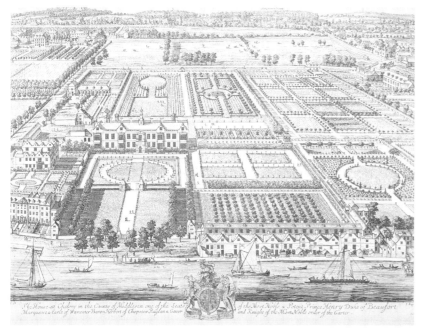

Adrenalin Village (far left) at the southern end of Chelsea Bridge, provides bungee-jumping from its 90-metre (300-foot) high crane which swings its victims out over the water before they take the plunge, usually with a blood-curdling shriek. Westminster Sailing Club offers a more sedate form of recreation on the river.

Chelsea was once a 'Village of Palaces': Kip's aerial view of 1720 (left) shows the Duke of Beaufort's house and gardens on the river front, where Sir Thomas More once lived. Today Beaufort Street runs down to meet Cheyne Walk at Battersea Bridge.

In 1682 Charles II commissioned Sir Christopher Wren to design the Royal Hospital in Chelsea (above), to provide a refuge for army veterans. Chelsea Pensioners in their traditional uniforms (blue for everyday and scarlet for special occasions) are still a familiar sight in the streets of Chelsea.

house to the east of the hospital buildings. A famous musical event took place near here in the summer of 1717, when George Frederic Handel's *Water Music* received what was probably its first public performance. Handel, who had worked for the King in George's native Hanover, followed his royal master to London, and wrote the suite to provide the musical backdrop to a royal excursion on the Thames. A contemporary account describes how the King and several ladies 'took Water at Whitehall in an open Barge' and set off for Chelsea. There was a second barge 'wherein were 50 instruments of all sorts, who play'd all the Way from Lambeth … the finest Symphonies, compos'd express for this Occasion by Mr Hendel which his Majesty liked so well, that he caus'd it to be plaid over three times in going and returning.' The barges 'drove with the Tide without rowing as far as Chelsea' where the party disembarked to eat supper at Lady Ranelagh's villa.

In 1742, thirty years after Ranelagh's death, the pleasure gardens bearing his name opened on the site, and were an instant success. By 1744 Horace Walpole was going 'every night constantly to Ranelagh, which has totally beat Vauxhall. Nobody goes anywhere else, everybody goes there.' It was the place to be seen, as Dr Johnson explained: 'Yes, Sir, there are many happy people here. There are many people here who are watching hundreds, and who think hundreds are watching them.' The great attraction of Ranelagh was the Rotunda, designed by William Jones. A round domed building, on the outside it looked like a smaller Royal Albert Hall; the inside was brilliantly lit by thousands of candles, and there were two tiers of

galleries. Ranelagh was famous for its music, which reached its height in the 1760s when Thomas Arne was in charge. He regularly performed his own music as well as works by Handel; and in 1761 a concert was advertised, to be given by 'the celebrated and astonishing Master MOZART… a child of 7 years of age … justly esteemed the most extraordinary Prodigy, and most amazing Genius that has appeared in any Age'. The Rotunda was demolished in 1805, and the grounds of Ranelagh House were returned to the Royal Hospital. Today they form the part of the gardens lying between Chelsea Bridge and the hospital.

To the west of the hospital are the high walls of the Chelsea Physic Garden, founded by the Apothecaries' Company in 1676. The first heated greenhouse in England was built here five years later, and cedar trees from Lebanon were planted which lived for more than 200 years. There is a large collection of medicinal plants and herbs, as well as shrubs and trees from all parts of the world.

To the left of the Physic Garden is Cheyne Walk: nowadays this is hidden from the river by the Chelsea Embankment, but originally the river came close to the houses, and was kept at bay by a low river wall. Cheyne Walk, with its surrounding streets, has had many famous and distinguished inhabitants. It included the site of Sir Thomas More's house and Henry VIII's old Chelsea Manor House. In the early eighteenth century these were demolished to make way for the home of Sir Hans Sloane, who gave his name to Chelsea's famous square and his collection of antiquities to the nation. Sloane's bequest formed the nucleus of the British Museum.

Mozart once played in the Rotunda at Ranelagh Gardens in Chelsea (left), built by William Jones in the 1740s. The site is now in the grounds of the Royal Hospital. This engraving is after a painting by Canaletto.

Battersea Bridge (far right) is a handsome dark green structure built by Sir Joseph Bazalgette in the late 1880s. The spandrels are picked out in gold, and the balustrades are made up of pairs of columns in an elegant Moorish design.

The Duke of Wellington and Lord Winchilsea both aim to miss during their duel on Battersea Fields in 1829 (right). The caricature is a reference to Wellington's military career; British soldiers were known as 'redcoats' or 'lobsters'.

In the next century Oscar Wilde, George Eliot and Thomas Carlyle all lived on or near the river in Chelsea; George Eliot came here hoping the mild air would be good for her health, but died within nineteen days of moving in. Carlyle's house in Cheyne Row, which now belongs to the National Trust, is almost unchanged since he lived, worked and entertained here from 1834 until his death in 1881. The painters Dante Gabriel Rossetti, Joseph Mallord Wiliam Turner, James Abbott McNeill Whistler and John Singer Sargent all lived or had studios near here. Whistler painted many evocative *Nocturnes* of the river, and made a series of etchings of Old Battersea Bridge before it was rebuilt in the 1880s. Whistler took two local boatmen, Henry and Walter Greaves, under his wing and gave them painting lessons in return for excursions on the river. Walter Greaves imitated his master's style both in his painting and in his trademark costume of top hat and white gloves. Whistler's friendship, which later turned to enmity, with Oscar Wilde dates from the time they both lived here. Wilde enjoyed Whistler's flashes of wit and was not above using them in his own conversation. He once praised Whistler for some particularly happy expression by saying, 'Ah, I wish I'd said that.' 'You will, Oscar, you will!' came the devastating reply. In 1846 Turner took lodgings with a Mrs Booth at the far end of Cheyne Walk. He lived in Chelsea for most of the last five years of his life and insisted on being known as Mr Booth, in an attempt to remain anonymous. He became known locally as Admiral or 'Puggy' Booth, and spent much of his time watching and painting the river. He would often hire a boat, usually from Charles Greaves, father of Whistler's

boatmen, and liked to be rowed over to St Mary's Church in Battersea to watch or sketch the river from the oriel window over the west door.

The stretch of the south bank between Chelsea Bridge and Albert Bridge is occupied by Battersea Park. Battersea means Beaduric's Eye or Island, in the sense of a slightly higher piece of land rising above low-lying marshes. In the early nineteenth century the nearby Red House Tavern became notorious for attracting a criminal clientele. Battersea Fields provided a discreet place for gentlemen to settle their disputes. In 1829 the Duke of Wellington was involved in a duel with Lord Winchilsea; neither was hurt as both deliberately fired wide. Gypsy camps were set up on the fields of Battersea, and on Sundays there was a rowdy fair with donkey races, conjurors, acrobats and stalls selling liquor. To suppress these unseemly activities Battersea was converted into a Royal Park in 1853. The designs for the new park were by Sir James Pennethorne. The level of the ground was raised above the marshes with earth dug out during the creation of the Royal Victoria Dock in the East End; more than a million cubic feet of earth were shipped by barge along the river. Thousands of exotic plants and shrubs were planted, many coming from Kew Gardens; there are also paths and a serpentine lake. In 1951 the Festival of Britain Gardens were laid out in the park to designs by Osbert Lancaster and John Piper; attractions included firework displays, a crazy railway designed by the *Punch* cartoonist Emmett, a tree walk and a funfair. As a small boy living in Chelsea at the time I vividly remember crossing Chelsea Bridge to visit the gardens; I particularly liked the tree walk, a precarious gangway strung between

the tops of trees. I felt quite safe, although I wasn't at all happy crossing Chelsea Bridge; I was always afraid it would collapse under my weight and throw me into the Thames. A Buddhist Peace Pagoda was built overlooking the river in 1985.

Just before the Albert Bridge, a covered jetty or walkway leads down from Chelsea Embankment to Cadogan Pier, where I have kept my boat over the three years I have been preparing the photographs for this book. It is one of the very few pontoons with public mooring spaces available on the river. The advantage of a floating pontoon is that there is enough water to set sail whatever the state of the tide, as the whole pontoon simply rides up and down with the tide; and the walkway, hinged to follow the movements of the pontoon, means that it is always accessible from the land. If you moor a boat to a buoy in the river you need a tender to get to it; and if you leave it pulled up on the bank you have to wait for the tide before you can get off. The various marinas along the river are also only accessible at high tide, as the locks in and out of them can be opened only when the difference in water level between the river and the marina is at a minimum. The present pier replaced an early nineteenth-century one which had two towers with a suspension bridge hanging from chains between them.

Cadogan Pier is almost under Albert Bridge, a three-span bridge designed by R. M. Ordish in 1873. The most elegant of all the bridges across the Thames is a hybrid design, half cantilever and half suspension bridge. The suspension elements hang from ornamental cast-iron towers with Gothic details painted in pink and pale blue. At night hundreds of light bulbs give it a fairground look. There are little octagonal huts resembling pepper pots at both ends of the bridge; these are the original toll booths. They are a reminder that most of London's bridges were built as commercial concerns, and charged for making a crossing until they were bought out by the Metropolitan Board of Works in the late 1870s. The freeing of the bridges was a great event: in 1879 the Prince and Princess of Wales spent the Queen's birthday driving across all the recently freed bridges, including the Albert Bridge. The original structure was weakened by the increasing weight of traffic, and in the 1960s there were plans to demolish it. Public protests led to its reprieve, and in 1971 the central span was strengthened by the addition of a pair of central piers. There is a notice requiring troops crossing the bridge to 'break step' to avoid damaging the structure. To the west of Albert Bridge, on the south bank, are the offices of Foster Associates, Sir Norman Foster's architectural practice. With its windows of pale green glass, his streamlined modern design of 1990 owes nothing to the fashionable post-modern vocabulary of primary colours and classical elements. The bottom three floors are studios; above this are four floors of flats, with penthouse suites at roof level.

Within a quarter of a mile of Albert Bridge we come to the cast-iron Battersea Bridge, a handsome dark green structure with five arches, built by Sir Joseph Bazalgette in the late 1880s. This replaced an earlier bridge designed by Henry Holland in 1771: with no less than sixteen

Sir Norman Foster's architectural practice (left) has its headquarters in this modernist block at Battersea.

Old Chelsea Bridge (far left), built in the 1850s, was replaced by the present bridge in the 1930s.

The Albert Bridge in Chelsea (right) was built by R. M. Ordish in 1873. It is a three-span design, with ornamental cast-iron towers and Gothic details painted in pink and pale blue. Its elegant form is picked out at night by hundreds of light bulbs.

wooden piers sticking out of the water like bundles of sticks, this was a serious hazard to navigation. Old Battersea Bridge inspired Whistler and Greaves to some of their most evocative work. On the north Chelsea bank, just before Battersea Bridge is Crosby Hall, which is being restored to recreate a Tudor palace on the Thames. Crosby Hall was originally in Bishopsgate in the City; it was demolished in 1908, but the interiors were saved and re-erected in Chelsea on the former site of Sir Thomas More's garden. The new exterior is a riot of patterned brickwork, pointed gables, oriel windows and lead cupolas. On the other side of Battersea Bridge is a cluster of houseboats permanently moored under Chelsea Embankment; residents can live on the river all year round, and they enjoy the prestige of a postal address in Cheyne Walk. One of the houseboats (see page 5) is the former barge belonging to New College, Oxford, and still has its galleried viewing platform and the college coat of arms on the prow. Similar college barges were used at rowing regattas at Henley and Oxford and other events on the river (see page 52).

Beyond the houseboats, at the mouth of Chelsea Creek, is Lots Road Power Station, which supplies the London Underground system with much of its power. Arnold Bennet paid a visit in 1913: 'I came to a gigantic building, quite new to me – a building which must be among the largest in London, a red brick building with a grandiose architectural effect, an overpowering affair, one of those affairs that man creates in order to show how small and puny he himself is'. It was built in 1902–5 on land occupied by the former Cremorne Gardens. These pleasure gardens had opened in the 1840s, almost forty years after Ranelagh Gardens had closed and when Vauxhall was approaching the end of its life. The attractions included an American bowling-saloon, a theatre and a banqueting hall; the crowds were entertained by military pageants, musical performances and the occasional balloon ascent. One flight had a disastrous outcome when the balloon floated towards the nearby church of St Luke and got snagged on the spire, killing the pilot. The gardens closed in 1877. St Mary's Church, Turner's favoured retreat, faces Lots Road Power Station from the south bank.

Beyond the power station, on the north bank, is Chelsea Harbour, designed in the 1980s for the shipping company P & O by Ray Moxley, who drew inspiration from the 'Ships, towers, domes, theatres and temples… open… to the sky' celebrated by Wordsworth's poem *Composed upon Westminster Bridge, September 3, 1802*. The development is centred on the marina with mooring facilities for luxury yachts; there are also seven restaurants and bars, and a health club which achieved brief notoriety in the mid-1990s when the Princess of Wales was secretly photographed working out in the gym. The three glass domes to the left house a design centre, and the complex is dominated by the pagoda-like belvedere tower with a 'tide ball', a gold ball which moves up and down a pole to indicate the state of the tide.

To the left of St Mary's, on the site of the old Hovis Factory, a new development is being built. Designed by Richard Rogers, Montevetro is another example of luxury high-rise housing on the river, and will provide an interesting contrast to the bleak public sector tower blocks overshadowing St Mary's.

St Mary's, Battersea (left), was built in 1775–7. It was a favourite haunt of J. M. W. Turner, who used to come here to sketch the river from the oriel window over the west door. It is unhappily overshadowed by some of the worst high-rise housing of the 1960s.

Chelsea Harbour (right) was designed in the 1980s for the shipping company P & O by Ray Moxley. It has a marina with mooring facilities for luxury yachts, as well as seven restaurants and bars. The development is dominated by the pagoda-like belvedere tower with a 'tide ball', a gold ball which moves up and down a pole to indicate the state of the tide.

Wandsworth to Hammersmith

Wandsworth, Fulham, Putney and Hammersmith

As we go under Battersea Railway Bridge and leave Chelsea for Wandsworth, the river changes character and briefly becomes more industrialized. On the south bank is Westland Heliport, situated on the Thames because single-engine helicopters flying over London have to follow the course of the river to avoid crashing onto a residential area in the event of engine failure.

Wandsworth Bridge was built in 1936–40 by Sir T. Pierson Frank, replacing an earlier bridge of 1870 by J. H. Tolmé. For river traffic the bridge marks the beginning of a speed limit of eight knots enforced by the launches of the Thames River Police and the Harbour Master. On the south bank before the bridge is a distillery, and beyond the bridge is Young's Wandsworth Brewery which, with its strong smell of malting barley, continues a tradition of brewing on the banks of the Wandle since the sixteenth century. The Wandle is the largest tributary of the Thames in London. The Fleet, the Westbourne and the Tyburn have all disappeared or been transformed into sewers, but the Wandle still flows into the Thames at Wandsworth. It no longer drives watermills to grind flour, or provides water for the once famous Wandsworth hat industry, which used to supply the cardinals in Rome with their distinctive red headgear. In recent years a number of factories, such as the Blue Circle Cement Works have been demolished and replaced by housing estates and supermarkets.

Beyond the Wandle the character of the Thames becomes more rural. For the first time there are parks on both banks: Wandsworth Park on the south and Hurlingham Park on the north. Through the trees at the water's edge we can glimpse Hurlingham House, built in the 1760s. This is the home of the Hurlingham Club, associated with many sporting activities, especially polo. The club devised the rules for the game in the 1870s, but it lost its polo grounds when they were compulsorily purchased to make way for council housing. The river, which has followed a south-westerly course since Battersea Bridge, now turns north-west as it heads to Hammersmith Bridge. As it does so, it passes the ancient villages of Putney and Fulham, whose parish churches face each other across Putney Bridge. In 1724 Daniel Defoe, in his *Tour through England and Wales*, makes the point that London used to be a series of villages: 'from Richmond to London, the river sides are full of villages, and those

Hurlingham House (above), can be glimpsed through the riverside gardens.

The parish churches of Putney and Fulham face each other across Putney Bridge (left). Built in 1729, for twenty years this was only river crossing in central London besides London Bridge. In the 1880s the wooden bridge was replaced by Sir Joseph Bazalgette with the present five-span granite structure.

Wandsworth Bridge (right) was built in 1936–40 by Sir T. Pierson Frank. I was glad to be within easy reach of my moorings in Chelsea when this storm blew up.

villages are so full of beautiful buildings, charming gardens and rich habitations of gentlemen of quality that nothing in the world can imitate it.'

In prehistoric and Roman times this stretch of the river was non-tidal; and it is the only place between the Strand in the east and Richmond in the west where gravel terraces led down to the water's edge. These gravel terraces were formed by the action of the river over many thousands of years. About two million years ago, the Thames followed a completely different course, running some forty miles to the north-west through the modern Vale of Aylesbury. The spread of glaciers at the onset of the Ice Age diverted the river southwards, until about a quarter of a million years ago it had settled into more or less its present course, carving out the Thames Valley in the process. The river was then much wider, and sea levels higher; as sea levels changed, the river cut deeper and deeper channels, a process accelerated by increasing quantities of water flowing down the river as the ice caps melted. In doing so its former flood plains were left behind as terraces; examples of these 'flood plain terraces' can still be seen at Chelsea Hospital and Trafalgar Square.

In Putney the gravel at the water's edge provided a firm footing for a river crossing, and the river was probably shallow enough to be fordable. The higher land on the south bank was free from the danger of flooding, making Putney an ideal place for early human settlement. There are many archaeological remains in this area, particularly flint blades and axes from the Neolithic period (4500 to 2200 BC). The Iron Age, which lasted roughly from 700 BC

to the arrival of the Romans, has also provided a number of finds of daggers and sheaths, many in the Thames itself. There are also numerous finds of Roman coins and pottery. Putney is important enough to be recorded in the *Domesday Book* of 1086, and from this period on both Putney and Fulham had many orchards, market gardens and nurseries, which exported their produce along the river to feed the cities of Westminster and London. In 1750 William Charlwood had several dozen acres in Putney on which he grew thirty-seven plants, including tulips, garlic, asparagus and strawberries; much of this was sold from his stand in Covent Garden Market. There were also important fisheries for salmon and eels in this stretch of the river. By the seventeenth century one householder in three in Putney made his living as a waterman. An important ferry operated between Putney and Fulham, and ferries also ran to Westminster and the City: the thirteenth-century account books of Edward I show Robert the Ferryman being paid to take the King and his family to Westminster.

In 1729 a wooden bridge was built to connect Putney and Fulham; this was the first river crossing west of London Bridge until the construction of Westminster Bridge in 1750. The wooden bridge was replaced by Sir Joseph Bazalgette in 1882–6 with the present five-span granite structure, today the busiest of all the London bridges. On the north bank Fulham Palace is set in twenty-seven acres of gardens known as the Bishop's Park. The palace,

The University Boat Race of 1996 ended in another win for Cambridge. Here the crews pass under Hammersmith Bridge (left).

The University Boat Race passes under a crowded Hammersmith Bridge (far left) in this engraving by Gustav Doré in 1877.

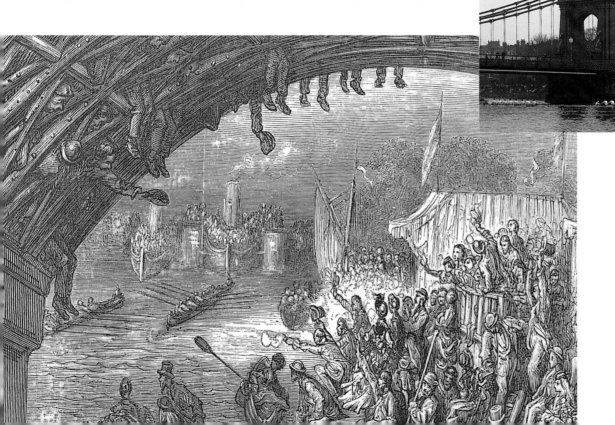

hidden from the river by the trees of the park, was the home of the Bishops of London until 1973. Although the bishops had probably had a house here since the eleventh century, the present brick building dates from the early sixteenth century. Beyond the park are the grounds of Fulham Football Club, owned by Mohammed Al-Fayed, the proprietor of Harrod's.

Near Putney Bridge is the first of the two University Stones, which mark the starting and finishing points for the University Boat Race between Oxford and Cambridge. The race runs between Putney and Mortlake, along a course first used for the sculling championships of England: this was a professional race which attracted a large public, and many bets were placed on the results. Further downstream the river was usually too crowded to be used for rowing events, although the most famous professional contest, Doggett's Coat and Badge Race, runs from London Bridge to Chelsea. Thomas Doggett was an Irish actor and theatre manager who set up the race in 1716 for recently qualified watermen; the winner receives a splendid red coat with a large silver badge on the arm. The race is still held every summer.

As rowing became a popular sport during the nineteenth century, professional events were replaced by amateur competitions. From the 1850s several rowing clubs were established at Putney, including the famous Leander Club which had a boathouse here from 1860 until the Second World War. On the south side Putney Embankment has a series of boathouses with slipways where boats can be launched into the water.

For the next mile and a half leading up to Barn Elms Reach, the river is mostly residential on the Fulham side. On the Putney side the river has a rural aspect: there are sports grounds with trees overhanging the water, followed by the green banks separating the river from the large reservoirs of Barn Elms. Beyond the reservoirs is Harrod's Depository, built for customers of the Knightsbridge emporium to store their belongings. The building dates from the 1890s; with its cupolas and red terracotta tiles, it is reminiscent of the main shop. Across the river are the striking offices of the Richard Rogers Partnership, converted from an old warehouse in the mid-1980s. Below the new barrel-vaulted steel roof, the semi-circular window is protected from the afternoon sun by yellow blinds which unfurl like sails. In the courtyard is the River Café, a glamorous restaurant in an elegant setting, which is owned and run by Ruth Rogers and Rose Gray. To the north are three blocks of flats, also part of the Rogers development; these are typical examples of mid-1980s residential design, with balconies enclosed within stainless steel, looking a little like supermarket trolleys without wheels. Some 180 metres (200 yards) beyond the flats is Riverside Studios, now a television studio and arts centre; in the 1930s and '40s it was a film studio belonging to the matinee idol Jack Buchanan.

For five or six miles between the Putney and Kew Bridges, the river meanders through another pair of loops: the first loop encloses Barnes on the south bank, the second Hammersmith and Chiswick on the north. Hammersmith Bridge is another example of Sir Joseph Bazalgette's work, and this too replaced an earlier bridge; the

Harrod's Depository at Barnes (right) was built in the 1890s. It is now being converted into flats.

In 1996 the European Football Cup finals were held in England; this giant model of the cup (far right) was paraded on the river as a publicity stunt. In the background is Thames Wharf, where the Richard Rogers Partnership, in conjunction with Lifschutz Davidson Design, created their impressive offices. The semi-circular window is protected by yellow blinds which unfurl like sails. The celebrated River Café is on the ground floor.

original, built in 1827, was the first suspension bridge in London. Bazalgette's is also a suspension bridge with supporting towers of decorative cast iron, painted dark green with gold detailing; he incorporated the old piers and abutments into his design. The bridge provides a grandstand view of the University Boat Race, and as the crews pass underneath they know they have covered roughly two-fifths of the course. The bridge used to be packed with spectators until a few years ago when it was closed by the police on the grounds that it was too crowded. In the middle of the bridge, on the Chiswick side, is a bronze plaque on the handrail; it commemorates the bravery of Lieutenant Wood of the RAF from South Africa, who died after diving into the river from the bridge to save a woman from drowning in 1919.

Beyond Hammersmith Bridge, there is a rustic walk along the south bank, lined with willows, poplars and willowherb. Behind the towpath are the playing fields and buildings of St Paul's School.

The original school, founded in 1509, was next to St Paul's Cathedral in the City; it moved to Hammersmith in the 1880s and to its present position in 1968. It has had many illustrious pupils, including John Milton, Samuel Pepys and, more recently, Isaiah Berlin. The north bank is one of the liveliest stretches of the river, and the first time where Londoners have easy access to their river. This is one of the most rewarding parts of the Thames Walk, with fine views of the river to the south and many interesting houses on the north. Just beyond Hammersmith Bridge is the pedestrian precinct of Lower Mall. The Rutland and the Blue Anchor are traditional pubs with outdoor tables overlooking the Thames. There are a number of rowing clubs and boathouses with walkways leading down to floating pontoons, and a cluster of houseboats in the river, including several canal narrow-boats moored side by side. On Boat Race Day the Lower Mall is packed solid with spectators, and the pubs do a roaring trade.

This was the site of Brandenburgh House, a splendid mansion and garden dating back to Charles I's time. Its most famous inhabitant was Caroline of Brunswick, the estranged wife of the Prince Regent. The arranged marriage between the first cousins had not been a great success: the first time he saw her the Prince Regent told his aide, 'Harris, I am not well, pray get me a glass of brandy'. There was a notorious scandal when the doors of Westminster Abbey were closed against Queen Caroline as she tried to attend her husband's coronation as George IV in 1821, and there was a public outcry when the government tried to strip her of her title and rights as Queen. Scores of watermen and lightermen mounted a demonstration in her support, packing the river at Brandenburgh House with their decorated barges; they presented an address to the Queen, to the accompaniment of cannon fire and music. Brandenburgh House was pulled down shortly after her death, within months of the coronation.

There are a number of rowing clubs along the embankment between Putney and Chiswick, with slipways where boats can be launched into the water (above). Many local schools offer rowing as a sport.

Hammersmith Bridge (left) was built in 1883–7, replacing an earlier suspension bridge. Another example of Sir Joseph Bazalgette's work, this is also a suspension bridge, with supporting towers of decorative cast iron, painted dark green with gold detailing.

Sailing boats (right) take part in a regatta at Hammersmith.

A little further along, Upper Mall has several fine Georgian houses overlooking the river. From 1877 to his death in 1896 William Morris lived at Kelmscott House, which he named after his Oxfordshire home, claiming 'the situation is certainly the prettiest in London'. With his friend and neighbour Sir Emery Walker, he established his printing and design works here. Their masterpiece

was *The Kelmscott Chaucer*, with its special typefaces, elaborate borders and ornamental capital letters which showed his love of natural forms of birds, flowers and trees, and his admiration for the decorative style of early book production. Although the products of the Kelmscott Press were only affordable by a rich elite, Morris was an ardent socialist who founded The Socialist League in 1884. The William Morris Society still occupies the basement of Kelmscott House, and visitors can see his printing press and some of his designs for fabrics and wallpaper. The house was built in about 1780. In 1816 Sir Francis Ronalds invented the electric telegraph here, laying miles of cable in the garden for his experiments. When he offered his invention to the Admiralty, he was told that in the aftermath of the Napoleonic War 'telegraphs are now totally unnecessary'.

The nearby Dove Inn dates from the seventeenth century; in 1796 it opened as the Dove Coffee House, which claims to be the place where James Thomson wrote the words for *Rule Britannia*. Linden House, an elegant early Georgian building with an Ionic portico, is the home of the London Corinthian Sailing Club; they have their own pontoon on the river and a flagpole on the waterfront used for signals to control regattas and races. Hammersmith Terrace, dating from the mid-1750s, is a fine row of seventeen houses with gardens leading down to the Thames; on the north side, away from the river, they have imposing Doric porches. There are several blue plaques commemorating distinguished residents, including Sir Emery Walker and the MP and author Sir Alan Herbert, whose novel, *The Water Gipsies*, is set on the river near Hammersmith.

Kelmscott House (above) on Chiswick Mall was built in about 1780. William Morris lived here from 1877 to his death in 1896, and established his design workshop and printing press on the premises. One of the works produced here was *The Kelmscott Chaucer*. The William Morris Society occupies the basement.

Linden House (right) on Chiswick Mall is the elegant early Georgian home of the London Corinthian Sailing Club.

Denizens of Hammersmith houseboats (far right) relax over their Sunday papers on a sunny morning. With Chelsea, this is one of the few places on London's river with permanent residential moorings.

Hammersmith to Kew

Chiswick, Barnes, Mortlake, Strand on the Green and Kew

Beyond Hammersmith Terrace is Chiswick Mall, a succession of elegant seventeenth- and eighteenth-century houses. This part of the river is prone to flooding; the houses all have flood doors and their garden walls are topped by 30 centimetres (1 foot) or more of thick glass to keep the water back. In the seventeenth century Walpole House was the home of Charles II's favourite mistress, Barbara Villiers, Duchess of Cleveland, 'the fairest and the lewdest of the Royal concubines'; by the early nineteenth century it had become a school. Thackeray was a pupil and he is said to have used Walpole House in *Vanity Fair* as the model for Miss Pinkerton's Academy, where Becky Sharp disdainfully throws away Dr Johnson's *Dictionary*. More recently the Redgrave acting dynasty lived at Bedford House. On the river front the houses along Chiswick and Upper Mall have delightful gardens, with many willow trees, magnolias, lavender hedges and even a palm tree.

This stretch is popular with recreational users, and rowing crews and single sculls are a common sight in Chiswick Reach all year round. For the next mile and a half the river turns south-west again as it heads towards Mortlake: Barnes nature reserve is on the left, while on the right is Chiswick Eyot or Ait. At high tide this is an island on the north side of the river, but at low tide it is accessible from the north bank. It is about 270 metres (300 yards) long, and covered with osiers, or pollarded willow trees, once harvested for making baskets. The eyot used to be longer, but has been eroded by the tidal action of the river. The local council threatened to demolish it completely, as the debris was a nuisance to river traffic. After a local outcry it was saved by having its banks reinforced with concrete blocks in the 1980s. It too is now a nature reserve, and there have been reported sightings of a seal and a dolphin near the island. There was probably an early settlement here, as flint tools and pottery from about 4500 BC have been found on the eyot. There are several of these tidal islands between here and Kew; originally there were many more gravel outcrops in the river, but most have been submerged by changing water levels, or have been built over. The remaining eyots give us a good idea of what areas like Thorney Island (Westminster) and Southwark must once have been like.

In the Middle Ages Chiswick belonged to the Bishop of London's Fulham estates; it is not mentioned in the *Domesday Book*. The name may refer to a 'cheese farm'. The early village developed around the riverside parish church of St Nicholas, the patron saint of sailors and fishermen, reflecting Chiswick's origin as a fishing community. The group of houses between the church and the river

Hammersmith Terrace (left) is an elegant row of mid-eighteenth-century houses, with gardens leading down to the river.

Chiswick Bridge (right) was built in 1933 to Sir Herbert Baker's designs, and carries the Great Chertsey Road (A316) towards the south-west. The nearby University Stone marks the finishing point of the annual Boat Race.

was originally called 'Slut's Hole', so perhaps Chiswick was once known for other attractions; in the 1860s the name was changed to Fisherman's Place. From 1749 to 1764 William Hogarth had a house nearby, his 'little country box', 'close to that amiable creature, the Thames'. His tomb in St Nicholas's churchyard is inscribed with a verse by his friend David Garrick:

> *Farewell, great Painter of Mankind*
> *Who reach'd the noblest point of art …*
> *If Genius fire thee, Reader, stay,*
> *If Nature touch thee, drop a Tear;*
> *If neither move thee, turn away,*
> *For Hogarth's honour'd dust lies here.*

Inside the church Lord Burlington is buried in his family vault; his friend and protégé William Kent lies next to him. He met Kent while on a Grand Tour in Italy and brought him back to England, installing him in an apartment in Burlington House, now part of the Royal Academy, in London. Together they established the Palladian style in architecture, which set the standard for good taste amongst the English aristocracy for a generation or more. The Palladian movement turned away from the Baroque extravagance of Wren, Vanbrugh and Hawksmoor, and looked back instead to the austere purity of Inigo Jones, and from him to the architecture of Renaissance Italy and classical antiquity. It is ironic that Hogarth, who so disliked and despised the new style, which he regarded as a foreign intrusion, should be buried so close to its high priests. He particularly disliked William Kent; they had attended the same painting academy,

leading Hogarth to say 'never was there a more wretched dauber'.

One of the first examples of the new fashion, and the most celebrated building in Chiswick, is the villa built by Lord Burlington in 1725–9 and decorated with spectacular plaster ceilings by Kent. Early maps and engravings show the grounds of Chiswick House leading down to the river; nowadays the house is separated from the Thames by Burlington Lane and the Great Chertsey Road, carrying traffic towards Chiswick Bridge. As a painter Kent may have been, in Horace Walpole's waspish words, 'below mediocrity'; as a decorator and landscape gardener he triumphed. His design for the gardens of Chiswick House were the first example of a new naturalistic style that rejected the rigid parterres and complicated formal layouts popular in the seventeenth century. Instead it was based on the shimmering landscape paintings of Claude Lorrain, with cascades of water, open lawns and informal paths meandering through temples, sphinxes and obelisks. Walpole said: 'as a gardener Kent is the inventor of an art that realizes painting and improves nature', his genius was to see that 'all nature was a garden'. Although the gardens are much smaller than they were in Kent's time, a number of the garden buildings are still standing, including a gateway designed by Inigo Jones for Beaufort House in Chelsea. Burlington was responsible for the house itself, drawing inspiration from Palladio's Villa Rotonda at Vicenza. Both are square houses topped by shallow domes, with grand Corinthian porticoes reached by imposing staircases. At Chiswick there are two porticoes to Palladio's four; the one on the river front has an elaborate staircase once flanked by statues of Burlington's

This engraving of about 1750 shows the grounds of Chiswick House leading down to the river. Chiswick, built by Lord Burlington in 1725–9, was one of the first examples of the new Palladian school of architecture, while its gardens, designed by William Kent, started the fashion for a new naturalistic style of landscape gardening.

heroes, Palladio and Inigo Jones. When Burlington built the villa he had no intention of living in it; it was to be as a showcase for the new style, and a place to display his collection of furniture, paintings, sculpture and architectural books and drawings, many of which he had acquired while on his Grand Tour. It was here that he entertained his circle of friends, including Walpole, Pope, Swift and Handel, while he continued to live in a comfortable old Jacobean mansion just across the courtyard. This was demolished in the mid-eighteenth century when Chiswick passed into the hands of the Dukes of Devonshire. The 6th Duke, who inherited the house in 1811, kept a menagerie of exotic animals, including giraffes and an elephant. In 1828 Sir Walter Scott described Chiswick as 'dignified by the presence of an immense elephant, who under the charge of a groom, wandered up and down, giving an air of Asiatic pageantry'. The house became a private mental hospital in the 1890s, and was sold to the local council in 1928.

Chiswick House is the first of a series of houses and parks on the Thames which offered the royal family and powerful courtiers, as well as rich Londoners, a welcome retreat from the city. These estates were easily accessible by water, and in the plague years of the seventeenth century they became increasingly popular. They reached their height of fashion in the eighteenth century, and the golden years of English landscape gardening have left a rural legacy, as the parks of the old estates line the banks of the river. Chiswick House, Kew Palace, Syon House, Marble Hill House, Ham House and Hampton Court Palace: the list is an impressive rollcall of English architecture.

Recent housing developments at Chiswick Wharf and Regency Quay have kept the river front open, providing an enjoyable stretch of the Thames Path. The houses themselves are pleasant enough, but keen sailors will be particularly grateful to the developers for providing a pier where residents can moor their boats. They have even been thoughtful enough to allocate spaces for visiting craft – one of the few places on the river where it is possible to arrive by boat and go ashore for a meal. In 1864 heavy industry came to Chiswick when Thornycroft's shipbuilding yard opened at Church Wharf, specializing in fast steam-driven launches and torpedo boats. Eventually the boats became too big to manoeuvre past all the bridges on their way to the sea, and the factory moved to Southampton in 1909.

The river continues on a southerly course, with sports grounds on the right bank. On the left bank, there is a charming group of riverside houses at Barnes Terrace, one of which has a blue plaque identifying it as the home of Gustav Holst from 1908; the composer worked as the musical director of St Paul's Girls' School in Hammersmith. The terrace leads to Barnes Railway Bridge, the oldest surviving bridge below Richmond, built in 1846–9. Beyond the bridge on the south bank is Mortlake, famous in the seventeenth century for the tapestry works set up by Flemish weavers, which produced such celebrated pieces as those based on the Raphael Cartoons; the original cartoons and tapestries are now in the Victoria and Albert Museum. After the workshops closed in 1703, Mortlake made its living from a pottery, its market gardens and a large brewery on the river,

Barnes Railway Bridge (right) was built in 1846–9. Through the arch can be seen Barnes Terrace, where Gustav Holst lived from 1908; the composer was the musical director of St Paul's Girls' School in Hammersmith.

Hogarth's tomb (far right) in the churchyard of St Nicholas, Chiswick, next to the river.

which is still working today. The Thames loops to the north before passing under Chiswick Bridge. The bridge was built in 1933 to Sir Herbert Baker's designs; the nearby University Stone marks the end of the annual boat race (see page 93). Beyond the bridge on the left bank is a cemetery, followed by a succession of residential and industrial sites, including a lager brewery, a refuse depot and a sewage works. Chiswick Quay Marina is past the bridge on the right bank; its lock-gates open to allow boats through for a couple of hours either side of high water. About half a mile past the bridge on the right bank is Hartington Court, an Art Deco block of flats built in 1938. This is a long, low building, with a rectangular central tower rising through four storeys of brick, divided by sweeping bands of concrete balconies wrapped round the curved ends of the building. This land was once part of the Chiswick property of the Dukes of Devonshire: the Duke's oldest son is known as the Marquess of Hartington.

A quarter of a mile further on is Kew Railway Bridge; this elegant 1860s design by W. R. Galbraith is notable for the round-headed cast-iron piers supporting delicate lattice horizontal girders. Visible through the spans of the railway bridge is Strand on the Green, a pretty row of fine riverside houses and delightful gardens with mimosa, wisteria and roses. The houses

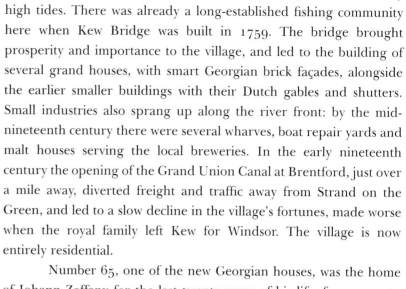

here need flood defences, as the river often overflows its banks at very high tides. There was already a long-established fishing community here when Kew Bridge was built in 1759. The bridge brought prosperity and importance to the village, and led to the building of several grand houses, with smart Georgian brick façades, alongside the earlier smaller buildings with their Dutch gables and shutters. Small industries also sprang up along the river front: by the mid-nineteenth century there were several wharves, boat repair yards and malt houses serving the local breweries. In the early nineteenth century the opening of the Grand Union Canal at Brentford, just over a mile away, diverted freight and traffic away from Strand on the Green, and led to a slow decline in the village's fortunes, made worse when the royal family left Kew for Windsor. The village is now entirely residential.

Number 65, one of the new Georgian houses, was the home of Johann Zoffany for the last twenty years of his life, from 1790 to 1810. Zoffany, the court painter to the Hanoverian kings, had an ostentatious lifestyle at Strand on the Green. His servants wore scarlet and he kept a pink and green sloop moored outside his house. When he gave musical evenings on the water, his friend and patron the Prince Regent liked to sit in a treehouse listening to the music. This was still a fishing community, and when Zoffany painted the Last Supper for St Anne's Church at Kew, local fishermen posed for the figures of nine of the Apostles. From then on they were known locally by their

Hartington Court (above) is a handsome Art Deco block of flats built in 1938.

Strand on the Green (left) is a row of fine riverside houses and delightful gardens with mimosa, wisteria and roses. Some (far right) have Dutch gables and gaily painted shutters.

The court painter Johann Zoffany lived in this fine Georgian house (right) from 1790 to 1810.

Apostle's name. Zoffany painted himself as St Peter, and his young wife as St John. He depicted as the traitor Judas a local lawyer with whom he had quarrelled about making his will, but 'Judas' was an important member of St Anne's community, and the church rejected the picture. It hangs instead in St Paul's, Brentford.

Distinguished residents of Strand on the Green have included Dylan Thomas and Nancy Mitford, who according to her sister Jessica had 'something of the aspect of an elegant pirate's moll', so she would have looked at home on the riverside. There are a couple of historic pubs here: the City Barge, dating back to 1497, is called after the Lord Mayor of London's barge which used to be moored here in the winter. At the Bull's Head there is a doubtful tradition that during the Civil War Oliver Cromwell escaped from the pub to the small island in the river called Oliver's Ait.

The first Kew Bridge of 1759 was built of wood; this was replaced by a stone bridge in the 1780s. The modern bridge was built of granite in 1903, to designs by Sir John Wolfe-Barry, the engineer in charge of the building of Tower Bridge. The Royal Botanic Gardens at Kew occupy the south bank for the next couple of miles; the garden was originally created by Frederick, Prince of Wales, and his wife Augusta, who lived here in the mid-eighteenth century. Augusta commissioned Sir William Chambers to adorn the gardens with several follies, including the famous Orangery and Chinese Pagoda. The park was landscaped by Capability Brown in the 1770s. Other important buildings were put up to house the growing collection of rare and exotic plants at Kew, initially created by Sir

Joseph Banks, who had accompanied Captain Cook on his Pacific journey of 1768. In 1841 the gardens were given to the nation, and three years later work started on the Palm House, designed by Decimus Burton and Richard Turner. The central section of this splendid conservatory has two tiers of curving glass walls leading to a central dome; the two wings are also curved, but a storey lower. In 1987 Diana, Princess of Wales opened the conservatory named in her honour; this is the largest glasshouse at Kew.

From the river the only building clearly visible is Kew Palace. Its gables and Flemish bond brickwork reflect the Dutch parentage of its original builder, Sir Samuel Fortrey. Built in 1631, it was known as the Dutch House until the royal family took it over in 1728; in 1802 it was occupied by George III, whose older children were taught 'practical gardening and agriculture' in the grounds. The river front at Kew Gardens is a screen of mixed trees, mostly oak, chestnut, sycamore and beech, giving the river a very rural character along this stretch (see page 5). The gardens are open to the public, and attract more than a million visitors a year. In the summer there are regular boat services from Westminster Pier. The belt of trees continues past the Old Deer Park, leading down to Richmond Bridge.

Returning to the north bank, a little to the west of Kew Bridge is the tall stand-pipe tower of the Kew Bridge Steam Museum, a former waterworks. The square brick tower, built in 1867, contains pipes up to 70.5 metres (235 feet) above ground. The function of these pipes was to receive water from the massive steam-driven engines in the plant, partly to maintain the pressure in the local

Kew Palace (left) is in the grounds of Kew Gardens. Built in 1631, it was known as the Dutch House until the royal family took it over in 1728.

Kew Railway Bridge (far right), designed by W. R. Galbraith in the 1860s. Visible through the bridge are a couple of riverside pubs at Strand on the Green. One of these is the Bull's Head. Local tradition claims that during the Civil War Oliver Cromwell escaped from this pub to Oliver's Ait (right) one of several small gravel islands in the river.

mains, and partly to protect the engines from a sudden loss of load in the event of a burst water main. One of the biggest engines, the Grand Junction 90, can be seen running at weekends when it is 'in steam'; the colossal beam engine has a cylinder diameter of 2.25 metres (90 inches), and pumps 2,148 litres (472 gallons) with each stroke. It helped to deliver West London's water supply for over a century. The museum also has a permanent display, *Water for Life*, dealing with the history of London's water supply from the Romans to the new underground Thames Water Ring Main.

The Thames has played a central role in this vital aspect of the city's life. The earliest settlements naturally gravitated to the river which, besides supplying water and abundant resources of fish, offered ease of movement and transport. The Romans were keen plumbers, and the museum has lengths of Roman clay pipe found in the City of London. From later periods there are small bore pipes made of lead, as well as larger wooden pipes, usually made from trunks of elm hollowed out and tapered to fit into each other. A branching section of trunk was used to divide the supply in two. Eventually these trunk pipes were laid along the major roads (giving rise to our expression 'trunk roads', hence 'trunk calls' on the telephone network).

In the early medieval period most of London's water supply came from springs and wells; in 1183 a commentator mentions the 'most excellent wells, whose waters are sweet, wholesome and clear'. With the increase in population and building density these supplies soon became inadequate, and conduits were installed to bring water from springs near Tyburn into the City. These supplies, originating on higher grounds, were fed by gravity, but as there was only a small drop in level from the source to the supply, the pressure was very low. There were also many leaks, so these conduits were inefficient, and in due course the local rivers became contaminated by sewage and industrial refuse from tanneries and breweries. Thames water was also used, but there was no mechanism for raising the water into the City until 1581, when Pieter Morice built his pump at London Bridge (see page 46).

This ability to pump Thames water up into the City revolutionized its water supply; henceforth the Thames would be one of the main sources of water for the growing city. In the reign of James I a new supply was established when a Welsh entrepreneur and goldsmith, Sir Hugh Myddelton, built his 'New River'. This channelled supplies from springs in Hertfordshire to reservoirs in Clerkenwell; from here wooden pipes carried it to the City, and smaller lead pipes took the supply to individual houses. A considerable length of the New River, from its source to Stoke Newington in North London, is still in use at the end of the twentieth century, while a disused section, home to several flocks of ducks and geese, survives in a public park at New River Walk in Islington.

By the middle of the nineteenth century a number of rival water companies were supplying London with water directly from the Thames but, as the river was also the city's main drain, pollution had reached dangerous levels. Robert Southey remarked in 1807: 'When it is considered that all the filth of this prodigious metropolis is

The mechanism of Pieter Morice's water-works at Old London Bridge (left) which pumped Thames water up into the City.

Kew Bridge links Middlesex and Surrey. This detail (right) shows Old Father Thames above three shields, taken from the seal of Surrey County Council. The chequered shield denotes the county of Surrey; the tower between two woolpacks is for the county town of Guildford; and the three salmon represent Kingston-upon-Thames, once famous for its fisheries.

emptied into the river, it is perfectly astonishing that any people should consent to drink it'. The development of the microscope showed that London water was teeming with microbes; as the Revd Sydney Smith wrote in 1834: 'He who drinks a tumbler of London water has literally in his stomach more than animated beings that there are Men, Women and Children on the face of the earth'. In his campaigning *Microscopic Examination of the Water supplied to the Inhabitants of London*, Arthur Hassall concluded that 'it is beyond dispute ... that a portion of the inhabitants of the metropolis are made to consume, in some form or other, a portion of their own excrement, and moreover, to pay for the privilege.' In 1854 John Snow proved that recent cholera outbreaks, which had killed 500 people in ten days, were caused by water taken from a polluted well. His 'coffin maps' showed the highest incidence of deaths clustered around a pump in Broad Street in Soho; this firmly established the connection between disease and water pollution, and demonstrated the need for pure water supplies.

In 1858, the year of the Great Stink (see page 64), Parliament was forced to act on the state of the Thames, resulting in the building of new interceptor sewers throughout London. The sewers were to catch the sewage before it reached the Thames, and where possible were housed in the new embankments being built at the same time. This successfully reduced the amount of sewage in the river; in any event, after 1856 the competing water companies were required to stop drawing their water from the tidal Thames. During the latter years of the nineteenth century, water treatment plants were built at Hampton and elsewhere which filtered the water through sand before it was put into the supply. The establishment of the Metropolitan Water Board in 1902 at last provided a unified management structure, and large reservoirs were built at Staines and Chingford. London finally had a clean and reliable water supply, which even survived the disruption caused by German bombing during the Blitz. During the early 1990s a new Thames Water Ring Main was built 40 metres (131 feet) below London to meet the increasing demand for water. A circular tunnel over 2.4 metres (8 feet) in diameter and 50 miles long, it is both a supply system and a reservoir holding 450 million litres (99 million gallons) of water. A section of the Ring Main is on show in the Steam Museum.

After Kew Bridge the river is divided by three islands, or aits, before it comes to Brentford and the entrance to the Grand Union Canal, linking London and Birmingham. For the first three miles the canal is really the River Brent, which gave its name to Brentford; the river was incorporated into the canal when it was created in the 1790s. The canal used to connect with the railways, but with the decline in canal traffic the Great Western Railway Dock has given way to a marina, with flats and houses. Waterman's Park occupies the site of a disused gasworks, and the Waterman's Arts Centre contains a cinema, theatre, restaurant and an exhibition gallery. Brentford has always enjoyed an important position at the junction of the main road to the west with a ferry across the Thames, and later with Kew Bridge. Nowadays the elevated section of the M4 Motorway thunders above the Great West Road at Brentford.

Kew Railway Bridge is in the foreground; in the distance is the tall stand-pipe tower, built in 1867, of the Kew Bridge Steam Museum. This former waterworks helped to deliver West London's water supply for over a century.

Kew to Richmond

Syon and Richmond

To the south-west of the Grand Union Canal lies Syon Park in Isleworth, the scene of two Battles of Brentford. In 1016 Edmund Ironside defeated King Cnut; the second battle was between Oliver Cromwell's Parliamentarians and the Royalists in 1642. The Royalists won the day, but were foiled in their attempt to retake London at the subsequent Battle of Turnham Green.

A nunnery had been here from the beginning of the fifteenth century, taking its name from the sacred hill of Sion in the Holy Land. When Syon was appropriated by Henry VIII in 1534, an outraged friar predicted that the King would be punished by having his blood licked by dogs. The macabre prophecy came true when Henry's coffin was brought to Syon to rest overnight on it way to Windsor; in the morning the servants found the coffin had burst open, and dogs were licking at his remains. During Edward VI's reign the Duke of Somerset acquired the land and embarked on building a house here: the present house follows his basic plan. After Somerset's execution the estate passed to the Duke of Northumberland. In 1553 Syon was the stage for one of the most tragic episodes in English history, when Northumberland attempted to stage a coup by placing his daughter-in-law, Lady Jane Grey, on the throne. She was only fifteen when she was offered the crown at Syon. She was taken downriver to the Tower,

and proclaimed Queen. After nine days the coup collapsed, and the conspirators met their end on the scaffold.

The property reverted to the Crown, and in 1594 Henry Percy, 9th Earl of Northumberland, acquired a lease from Elizabeth I; the Percys have owned Syon ever since. The earl's son engaged Inigo Jones to improve and embellish the house in the 1630s. In the 1660s John Evelyn visited Syon: 'I viewed that seat … builte out of an old Nunnerie, of stone, and faire enough; but more celebrated for the garden than it deserves; yet there is excellent wall fruit and a pretty fountaine, yet nothing extraordinarie'. In 1762 the 1st Duke of Northumberland considered the house 'ruinous and inconvenient', and commissioned Robert Adam to remodel it. Adam worked here for years, and although he kept to the basic plan of the Tudor house, its present appearance is mostly his work.

The house is built around a quadrangle that was the old monastic cloister, with a square tower at each corner, and battlemented outside walls. On the river front there is a stone lion over the central gateway that came from the family's mansion in the Strand, demolished in 1874. There are sumptuous interiors in the classical style of the late eighteenth century. Entrance rooms with black and white marble floors and green marble columns lead to the

108 LONDON FROM THE THAMES

The Picnic by F. W. Lawson (left).

Syon House (right), across the river from Kew Gardens, has been the property of the family of the Dukes of Northumberland since 1594. The house, built on the site of an old nunnery, was extensively remodelled by Robert Adam in the 1760s and '70s. The water meadow between the river and the house is a protected nature reserve, as the twice daily tidal flooding creates a very unusual habitat for several species, including the rare Hairy German Snail.

showpiece of the house: a grand drawing room with polychrome stucco ceilings, red silk wall hangings from Spitalfields and a carpet designed by Adam himself. In the grounds of Syon Park is a Regency conservatory, as well as a garden centre and rose garden. There are many beautiful and exotic specimens flying free inside the Butterfly House, opened in 1981. Syon House looks out towards the Thames across a broad expanse of water meadow, landscaped by Capability Brown between 1767 and 1773. This is a protected nature reserve, as the twice daily tidal flooding creates a very unusual habitat for several species, including the rare Hairy German Snail. In the southern corner of the park is the Pavilion, a delightful domed boathouse and lodge; when the Northumberlands travelled to Syon by water, this was where they landed.

As we leave Syon the river heads due south, passing All Saints Church, and the London Apprentice, a famous riverside pub which looks out onto Isleworth Ait. The ait, or island, is about half a mile long; it is another nature reserve, inhabited by bats roosting in boxes provided for them, as well as by herons. At low tide there is very little water on the west side, and the rare Two-Lipped Door Snail lives in the mud and shingle. The London Apprentice was popular with artists like Zoffany, Constable and Turner; Zoffany painted a portrait of his fellow artist Richard Wilson holding a tankard of porter in the pub. When Wilson, who pretended not to drink, took umbrage, Zoffany painted out the offending tankard.

As the river heads towards Richmond, it curves south-east, reversing its normal westward direction. For the next few miles, until Hampton Court, the river follows a broadly southerly course. The last couple of miles, with Kew and Syon facing each other across the river, are very rural; within a short distance the character of the river changes dramatically as we approach Richmond Lock and Weir. This was built in the 1890s, because improvements to the flow of the Thames downriver, particularly the building of the embankments in the 1870s, had reduced the river at Richmond to a muddy trickle at low tide. The lock is half-tidal, which means that at high tide boats can pass over the weirs; at low tide there is insufficient water on the downriver side, and the weirs become waterfalls as the level drops. To proceed upriver at low tide, light boats can be hauled out of the water and pulled over special rollers; heavier craft pay a few pounds to the lock-keeper to operate the lock and be lifted up by the water as the lock fills. Over the lock are a pair of recently restored elegant Victorian ironwork footbridges, reminiscent of railway architecture.

Upstream of Richmond Lock the river is maintained at a minimum depth of 1.7 metres (5½ feet), achieved by using sluice gates in the weirs to hold back the water when necessary. In a small boat it is noticeable how much more placid the Thames can be above Richmond Lock, as the river is no longer subjected to the full force of the ebb tide. But the river is not always gentle: after a bout of heavy rainfall the flow can be fast and furious. And the lock does nothing to protect against a rising tide; the stretch between Richmond and Teddington is prone to flooding at an exceptionally high tide. Twice a month the gravitational forces of the sun and the moon combine to produce a higher than usual 'spring' tide; and unwary car owners

Richmond Lock and Weir (left) was built in the 1890s. When I took this picture the lock had just emptied so that I could transfer my boat from the higher levels above the lock to the lower water below Richmond. The walls of the lock were still wet enough to catch the reflection of the setting sun, and the lock gates at the far end are opening to let me through.

Syon Pavilion (right) is at the south-western corner of the grounds of Syon House. When the Northumberlands travelled to Syon by water they landed at this delightful neo-classical boathouse and lodge.

who park near the river's bank at low tide can find their cars under water at high tide (see page 10).

In a short distance we reach Twickenham Bridge, designed by Maxwell Ayrton. In one sense this is a continuation of Chiswick Bridge, as both carry the Great Chertsey Road towards the M3 and the south-west, and both were built in 1933. Twickenham Bridge runs next to Richmond Railway Bridge, originally built in 1848 to connect Richmond to Windsor; the cast-iron bridge was replaced by the present steel structure in 1903. At the bridge, Isleworth gives way to Twickenham on the west (Middlesex) bank, while on the east (Surrey) side we move from Kew to Richmond.

Immediately on our left is the elegant Asgill House, built by Sir Robert Taylor in 1758 for Sir Charles Asgill. The river front has an octagonal bay breaking forward between two wings, and the roof lines of the bay and the wings combine to give the effect of a giant pediment. Asgill was a banker who rose to become Lord Mayor of London; he used the house to entertain his City friends, who arrived by river in the splendid barges of the livery companies (see page 52), complete with musicians. Asgill's son was a soldier fighting in the American War of Independence,

and was one of a group of officers taken prisoner. George Washington, as a reprisal for an outrage committed by the British army, ordered that one of the officers should die; they drew lots, and Asgill was chosen. His mother sent an impassioned plea to Louis XVI and Marie Antoinette to intercede with their American allies on Asgill's behalf. He was only spared after an Act of Congress was passed, and he returned to Richmond on lifelong parole.

Asgill House is at the end of Old Palace Lane, for this was once the river front of Old Richmond Palace, or Shene Palace as it was originally known. The name Shene, which could mean either 'shelter' or 'shining' in Anglo-Saxon, survives in several places in Richmond: Sheen Park, Sheen Road and East Sheen Common. The medieval palace of Shene was converted from an old manor house by Edward III, who died here in 1377. Shene became the favourite palace of Richard II and his wife, Anne of Bohemia; they held a lavish court here, daily feeding thousands of guests and retainers. Anne died of the plague at the palace in 1394 and her body was taken downriver to Westminster Abbey, where there is a powerful bronze effigy of her. Richard was so distressed that he ordered the destruction of Shene Palace; however, enough survived for it to be rebuilt by Henry V. When his buildings were gutted by fire in 1499, Henry VII rebuilt the palace once more, and re-named it Rychemonde after his Yorkshire earldom. Richmond Palace was Henry VII's favourite residence, and his sons, Arthur and the future Henry VIII, were largely brought up here. Henry VII died at Richmond, reputedly leaving hoards of gold hidden around the palace. His granddaughter Elizabeth I also died here in 1603; she had been very fond of Richmond, which she called her 'warm winter box'. The funeral procession taking her body from Richmond to Whitehall was described by William Camden:

> The Queen was brought by water to White-hall
> At every stroke the oars did tears let fall:
> More clung about the Barge, fish under water
> Wept out their eyes of pearl, and swam blind after.

After the execution of Charles I, most of the palace was destroyed. During the eighteenth century the royal family preferred Kew and Windsor, and Richmond Palace, once one of the glories on the Thames, was 'decayed and parcelled out in tenements'. All that survives of the palace is a Tudor gateway on Richmond Green with Henry VII's coat of arms and the restored Wardrobe buildings nearby.

Beyond Asgill House, Cholmondeley Walk is a pleasant tree-lined stretch leading to St Helena Terrace; the triumphalist name of this neo-classical row of houses recalls the island where Napoleon was exiled after his defeat at Waterloo. Further along the river is the 1980s

redevelopment of Richmond Riverside, a comprehensive rebuilding of the waterfront and the terrace above, carried out to the designs of Quinlan Terry. The style is traditional Georgian, and incorporates the façades of some earlier buildings facing the river, including Heron House (1716), Palm Court (1850) and Tower House (1856). Architectural purists and modernists condemn the whole thing as a pastiche, but Prince Charles was more impressed, seeing 'an expression of harmony and proportion'. It is certainly popular with the residents of Richmond, who on a sunny day throng the terraces leading down to the Thames; the granite and brick embankments, punctuated by steps and slipways, allow people to sit at the water's edge as they enjoy the river, watching their children paddle in the shallows.

Richmond Bridge, next to the Riverside, is London's oldest surviving bridge across the Thames. Built by James Paine and Kenton Couse in 1774–7 on the site of an old ferry crossing, the masonry bridge is faced with Portland stone. There are five spans with semi-circular arches, getting larger towards the middle as the bridge rises to a slight peak. Gilded lamps have been added to the balustrade. The bridge inspired a poem by Wordsworth:

> Glide gently, thus for ever glide
> O Thames! That other bards may see
> As lovely visions by thy side
> As now, fair river! come to me.

Asgill House, Richmond (above left) was built by Sir Robert Taylor in 1758 for Sir Charles Asgill, a banker who rose to become Lord Mayor of London. The recently restored house is on the site of the former Old Richmond Palace (left), originally known as Shene Palace, which was an important royal residence in the late medieval and Tudor periods. The palace was a particular favourite of Henry VII, and his granddaughter Elizabeth I died here in 1603. The palace was largely destroyed during the Commonwealth.

St Helena Terrace, Richmond (above). The name tells us that it was built in the years after Napoleon's defeat at Waterloo in 1815. St Helena is the small island where the fallen emperor was exiled.

Richmond Riverside (right) was comprehensively rebuilt in the late 1980s by Quinlan Terry. The style is traditional Georgian, and although it incorporates the façades of some earlier buildings, has generally been condemned as a pastiche by architectural purists and modernists. On the other hand, Prince Charles saw it as 'an expression of harmony and proportion'.

More energetically, Dickens boasted of 'swimming feats from Petersham to Richmond Bridge ... I myself have risen at 6 and plunged head foremost into the water to the astonishment and admiration of all beholders'.

In the summer, elegant old-fashioned rowing boats are moored in the middle of the river near Corporation Island. These are the sort shown in Victorian engravings where the passenger, usually a fashionable lady with elaborate headgear, controls the steering by handling a couple of tiller ropes connected to the rudder. Below Richmond Lock the tides run too fast for casual boating, so these rowing boats provide the first opportunity on the Thames for 'messing about in boats'; they can be hired from boathouses on either side of the bridge.

Once past the bridge we come to Petersham on the left bank before the river meanders to the west once more. There is an unconventional houseboat moored here, made up of a couple of old boats lashed together under sheets of tarpaulin; I have seen the owner throw breakfast parties for friends who row out to visit him with supplies of fresh milk.

After the built-up area around Richmond Bridge, we are now back in a rural environment with parks and lawns on both sides of the river. The view back towards Richmond is dominated by the Star and Garter Home. This colossal red brick building on a wooded escarpment of Richmond Hill replaced a famous hotel, built in

the mid-eighteenth century on land leased from the Earl of Dysart of Ham House; the name refers to the earl's membership of the Order of the Garter. The hotel flourished and in 1825 was described as 'more like the mansion of a nobleman than a receptacle for the public; looking down with stately aspect from the adjoining valley, and seen to advantage from every point of the horizon', where visitors could 'inhale the pure air and exhilarate their spirits by contemplating a wide-spreading circumference of rural scenery'. Among the regular visitors was Charles Dickens, who celebrated his wedding anniversary there every year with a dinner for friends. The hotel was rebuilt in the 1860s; the present building was designed by Sir Edwin Cooper in 1924. Since the First World War it has been a home for disabled servicemen.

The hotel's success owed much to the famous view of the Thames from the top of Richmond Hill, which in 1809 inspired one of J. M. W. Turner's finest landscapes, *Thomson's Aeolian Harp*. In 1727 James Thomson had described the scene in his poem *The Seasons*:

> *Heavens, what a goodly Prospect spreads around,*
> *Of Hills, and Dales, and Woods, and Lawns, and Spires,*
> *And glittering Towns, and gilded streams, till all*
> *The stretching Landskip into smoke decays*

The American William Byrd was so taken with the view that in 1733, when he returned to Virginia and founded a city overlooking the James River, he chose to call it Richmond. In *The Heart of Midlothian* of 1818

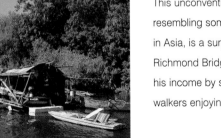

This unconventional houseboat (left), resembling something from a floating city in Asia, is a surprising sight so near to Richmond Bridge. The owner subsidises his income by selling duck eggs to walkers enjoying the Thames Path.

Richmond Bridge (above), with its five semi-circular arches encased in Portland stone, is London's oldest surviving bridge across the Thames. It was built by James Paine and Kenton Couse in 1774–7.

Sir Walter Scott's heroine comes to Richmond and admires the 'huge sea of verdure, with crossing and intersecting promontories of massive and tufted trees … tenanted by numberless flocks and herds, which seemed to wander unrestrained and unbounded through the rich pastures. The Thames, here turreted with villas and there garlanded with forests, moved on slowly and placidly.' In 1902 the view became the first to be protected by an Act of Parliament.

On the Twickenham side Marble Hill House, set in its large park, overlooks the Thames. The house itself is a fine Palladian villa built in the late 1720s for George II's mistress, Henrietta Howard, Countess of Suffolk. The designs were by Lord Henry Herbert, an amateur architect whose family owned Wilton House, Inigo Jones's masterpiece. Herbert was an enthusiastic Palladian and took as his starting point a design published by Colen Campbell in *Vitruvius Britannicus*, a publication which appeared between 1715 and 1725, promoting the new style with evangelical zeal. Herbert was helped in the construction of Marble Hill by Roger Morris. The house has five bays on the river side: the three central bays project forward beneath a pediment, the lines of which are repeated in the hipped roof. Henrietta Howard was fortunate to have Alexander Pope as a friend and neighbour, and with Charles Bridgman, the

royal landscape gardener, they laid out the park in the latest naturalistic style championed by William Kent at Chiswick (see page 100). The setting fulfilled Palladio's prescription for the ideal villa: 'advantageous and delicious as can be desired, being situated on a hillock of most easy ascent, at the foot of which runs a navigable river'. In this regard the situation was better than at Chiswick, with its relatively flat ground. The view from the house to the river was across an extensive lawn, and groups of trees were arranged to lead the eye to the Thames and Petersham Meadows beyond. By the late nineteenth century the house had been stripped of its contents and was in danger of falling down when the Cunard family rescued it for the nation. Restored in the 1960s, it is now a museum; in the summer the park is used for concerts. Unfortunately, the carefully contrived original view of the house from the river has been obscured by a screen of trees. The view through the one gap in the trees is spoilt by a permanently moored boat covered in blue tarpaulin; to get a shot worthy of the building I had to climb out of my boat and take a photograph from the towpath.

Across the river are Petersham Meadows and a strip of woodland known as Petersham Lodge Wood, containing an avenue of horse chestnuts surrounded by many mature trees. This area is rich in wild flowers, helped by the occasional flooding of the river; in the spring there are lesser celandine and lady's-smock, followed in the summer by meadow-sweet and meadow crane's-bill. There are also large populations of bats flourishing on the abundant insect life along the river.

The Star and Garter Home, Richmond (above). This colossal red brick building, which dominates the skyline above Richmond from upriver, was built by Sir Edwin Cooper in 1924. Since the First World War it has been a home for disabled servicemen.

Marble Hill, Twickenham (right), is a fine Palladian villa built in the late 1720s for Henrietta Howard, Countess of Suffolk, who was George II's mistress. It is now a museum, and in the summer the grounds are used for concerts.

Richmond to Hampton Court

Ham, Twickenham, Teddington, Kingston and Hampton Court

On the south bank, almost opposite Marble Hill is Ham House, one of the least altered seventeenth-century houses and gardens in the country. John Evelyn visited the house in 1678 and described it as 'furnished like a great Prince's; the Parterres, Flower Gardens, Orangeries, Groves, Avenues, Courts, Statues, Perspectives, Fountains, Aviaries, and all this at the banks of the Sweetest River in the World'. From the river we see the north front, with a statue of Old Father Thames in the courtyard. The house was originally built in 1610, by Sir Thomas Vavasour, a courtier of James I; in 1637 it was acquired by the Earl of Dysart. In his boyhood he held the unenviable position of being the whipping boy for the future Charles I: the prince's royal body could not be chastised when he misbehaved, so the punishments were inflicted on Dysart instead. Dysart's son-in-law was Lord Lauderdale, one of the famous ministry known as the Cabal (his initial supplying the last letter in the group's nickname). The ambitious and powerful Lauderdale enlarged the house in the 1670s, when it acquired more or less its present form. The outside of the house is dark red brick with stone dressings; the lavish interiors contain a fine collection of Stuart furniture and paintings. One of the house's principal treasures is the seventeenth-century formal garden mentioned by Evelyn. The National Trust now owns the house and grounds, and is restoring the garden. It is one of the few examples in the country to survive the eighteenth-century passion for landscape gardening started by William Kent at Chiswick (see page 100).

Another rare survival at Ham is a ferry service for foot passengers; Hammerton's Ferry runs between Petersham Meadows near Ham House on the south bank to Orleans Road near Marble Hill Park on the north, allowing architectural enthusiasts to travel easily between the two houses. Beyond Ham House, Ham Lands is a wild expanse crossed by avenues of limes planted by the Dysarts in the seventeenth century. This is a nature reserve for such rare species as the Nottingham catchfly; and with over 230 species of plants, including the scarce Deptford Pink, Ham Lands is one of the most important botanical sites in London. It also provides nesting sites for many birds, including tawny owls, woodpeckers and several species of warbler.

Opposite the nature reserve is the largest, and most quaintly named, island in the Thames: Eel Pie Island. Originally known as Twickenham Ait, this is a typical Thames ait or eyot (see page 36). It is high enough above the flood tides to be

There are many species of wild bird (left) to be seen on the upper reaches of the Thames in London, including herons, cormorants, swans and grebes. Here a pair of coots are building a nest amongst the moored boats at Eel Pie Island.

Ham House (right) is one of the least altered seventeenth-century houses and gardens in the country. One of the house's principal treasures is a seventeenth-century formal garden (far left), currently being restored by The National Trust. The Coade stone figure in the courtyard is a statue of Father Thames by John Bacon.

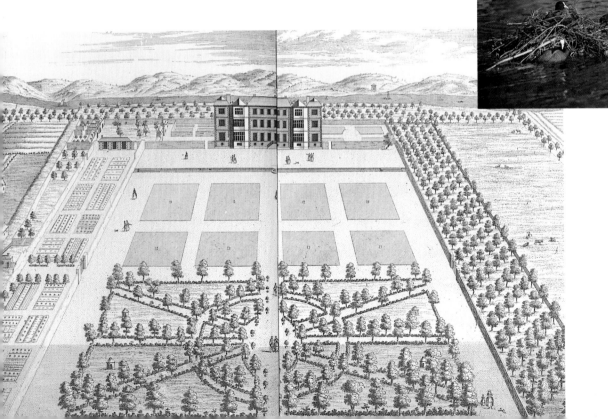

habitable, and has an eclectic collection of buildings, from bungalows to boathouses and boatyards accessible by a 1950s footbridge from the village of Twickenham. The jumble of busy boatyards gives the southern end of the island the look of a small ramshackle port. Until pollution and the demands of navigation put them out of business, there used to be several fish weirs in this part of the river, providing the eels for the pies which made the island famous. In *Nicholas Nickleby*, Dickens tells how one of the characters goes by steamer from Westminster to 'Eel-pie Island at Twickenham: there to make merry upon a cold collation, bottled-beer, shrub, and shrimps, and to dance in the open air'. No fish pies figured on this menu, although another writer, John Fisher Murray, describes a visit in 1853, when 'steamers are accustomed to land great numbers of holiday folks, desirous of the delights of pure air, and solicitous to banquet upon eel-pies'. Then the eels would have been imported from Holland, but today the pollution of the river has been drastically reduced, and eels are back in the Thames: I have seen a Great Crested Grebe dive for fish near the island and come up with an eel coiled round its beak. During a drought in 1884, before the lock at Richmond had been built to maintain water levels here, the channel between the island and Twickenham on the Middlesex bank dried up completely. Champagne parties were thrown to enjoy the novelty, as diners set up tables and chairs on the river bed; there was even a cricket match which drew hundreds of spectators.

On the Middlesex bank the medieval village of Twickenham is still discernible in the suburban sprawl, caused by the arrival of the trains after the railway bridge at Richmond was built in 1848. Alexander Pope is buried in the church of St Mary the Virgin, and on the outside wall the poet put up a plaque to his nurse 'in gratitude to a faithful old servant'. The church is behind a high brick wall to protect it from flooding. In his *Dictionary of the Thames*, Charles Dickens' son describes St Mary's as 'a sufficiently plain, not to say morose, building of red brick, with a redeeming point in the shape of its ivy embattled tower'. The main body of the church was rebuilt early in the eighteenth century, and the stone tower, now stripped of its ivy, dates from the fifteenth century. Nearby are the riverside gardens of York House, containing a very surprising fountain commissioned at the turn of the century by Sir Ratan Tata, a wealthy Indian. Very loosely inspired by Botticelli's *Birth of Venus*, this features a life-size group of naked ladies in a rocky setting, climbing provocatively in and out of the water.

The famous Twickenham Rugby Football Ground is a few minutes' walk from the river: there are a couple of busy pubs on the waterfront which do a lively trade on match days, as supporters tank up before and after the game. Further along the Twickenham shore is a long balustrade in front of the gardens of St Catherine's Convent; its tower is a landmark in this stretch of the river. We have reached the site of Pope's Villa, which used to be one of the most carefully contrived views from the Thames. Pope himself described it as rising 'high enough to attract the eye and curiosity of the passenger from the river, when, upon beholding a mixture of beauty and ruin, he inquires what house is falling, or what church is rising'. The poet had

The paddle steamer *Diamond* arriving at Twickenham (left). On the right is St Mary's Church, its earliest tower rising above the eighteenth-century nave.

Originally known as Twickenham Ait, Eel Pie Island (right) is high enough above the flood tides to be habitable. At the southern end busy boatyards gives the island the look of a small ramshackle port.

leased a house here in 1719, and commissioned a small Palladian villa from James Gibbs, where he lived for the last twenty-five years of his life. The garden, which he designed himself, became a famous example of the new style of gardening which Kent had started at Chiswick; its crowning glory was the grotto, 'finished with shells interspersed with pieces of looking-glass in angular forms, and in the ceiling a star of the same material.' By the early nineteenth century the villa and garden had attracted so many visitors that Sophia Howe, the exasperated owner, destroyed them, and today only parts of the grotto survive. For her vandalism she became known as 'The Queen of the Goths'. To accompany his painting of a *View of Pope's Villa at Twickenham*, Turner wrote:

> O lost to honor and the sence of shame
> Can Britain so forget Pope's well earned fame
> To desolation doom the poet's fane
> The pride of Twickenham's bower and silver Thame …

In his villa and garden Pope was seeking what he called 'the amiable simplicity' of the 'taste of the ancients'. He was trying to recreate the world of Cicero and Horace, whose poetry celebrated the contemplative tranquillity of life in a country villa; he nicknamed his house on the Thames 'my

Tusculum', referring to Cicero's villa outside Rome. In this Arcadian existence garden design was very important, and there was no room for the rigid formal planting an earlier generation had practised at Ham House. In 1731, in a letter to Lord Burlington, Pope set out his views on how to plan a garden:

> Let not each beauty ev'ry where by spy'd,
> Where half the skill is decently to hide.
> He gains all points, who pleasingly confounds
> Surprizes, varies and conceals the Bounds.

Three years after Pope's death in 1744, Horace Walpole bought the lease of what became Strawberry Hill, his famous Gothic castle set in a landscape garden overlooking the Thames, about half a mile beyond Pope's Villa. He described it as 'a little plaything of a house, the prettiest bauble you ever did see'. He was drawn to what he called 'Twickenhamshire' by its associations with Pope, and by the views of Twickenham, 'a seaport in miniature' which 'in the setting sun and the long autumnal shades enriched the landscape to a Claude Lorraine'. Walpole's garden followed Pope's and Kent's precepts, and in 1753 he planted 'a serpentine wood of all kinds of trees and flowering shrubs and flower'; a path meandered through the wood past a shell bench, an altar tomb, a Gothic gate and a Chapel in the Woods. In 1765 he wrote that 'the honeysuckles dangle from every tree in festoons; the syringas are thickets of sweets'. Except for the Chapel in the Woods, little is left of his garden today, but Strawberry Hill itself, with its celebrated Long Gallery, has survived being enlarged and transformed into a Catholic seminary. It is no longer

A boathouse at Eel Pie Island with decorative ironwork and diagonal use of clapboard (above). The owner told me it dates from 1905 and assured me that it doesn't suffer from the damp.

St James's School for Boys (right), with its distinctive half-timbered clock tower, dominates the waterfront at Twickenham, once the playground of Alexander Pope and Horace Walpole.

visible from the river, thanks to St James's School for Boys, with its distinctive half-timbered clock tower.

The river curves to the east as we leave the world of Pope and Walpole at Twickenham and head towards Teddington; on the Surrey side the open fields of Ham continue past Thames Young Mariners' Base, a watersports centre operating in a disused gravel pit with ten acres of water. One of the activities on offer is white-water rafting in the turbulent waters below Teddington Lock and Weir, about half a mile upstream. Teddington marks the limit of the tidal Thames; here control of the Thames passes from the Port of London Authority, who make no charge for using the river, to the National Rivers Authority, who charge several pounds a day for a licence. Amongst other things, the fee helps to finance the system of locks on the river. Teddington Lock allows access to the higher waters upstream, while the weirs control the flow of the river, which in times of flood can run to 68 billion litres (15 billion gallons) a day.

The lock and weir serve to cut off the Thames above Teddington from the effects of the tides, and to protect the nearby reservoirs at Molesey and Stain Hill from salt contamination. The absence of tides dramatically changes the character of the river for the last five miles of our journey to Hampton Court. Changes in river level are due to variations in rainfall; unless there has been a bout of heavy rain, the Thames now flows gently downstream. A new speed limit of four knots is in force, and there are many rowing, sailing and canoeing clubs in the waters above Teddington. There are also many more motor launches than in the tidal river, and in the summer

months a procession of these make the trip to Hampton Court and beyond, travelling at a stately pace. For the first couple of miles, from Teddington to Kingston Railway Bridge, the Thames Path follows a pleasant tree-lined walk along the south bank, while the north bank of the river is mostly lined with residential developments which were started in the 1860s when the railway arrived. Several of the houses in this stretch have elaborate boathouses at the water's edge.

Kingston Bridge was built of stone-faced brick by Edward Lapidge in the 1820s. On the Middlesex side the village of Hampton Wick is at the western end of the bridge. There has been a bridge across the river here since the Middle Ages; until the building of Richmond, Putney and Westminster Bridges in the mid-eighteenth century, Kingston Bridge was the first above London Bridge. The ancient town of Kingston-upon-Thames on the Surrey side owed much of its importance to its position at the bridgehead, and the name Kingston tells of its long-standing royal connections. Seven Saxon kings, including Alfred the Great, were crowned here, and it is the oldest of the three royal boroughs in the country, with a charter from King John in 1200. The usual riverside occupations of boat building, tanning, milling, brewing and malting were carried on here. The three salmon in Kingston's coat of arms reflect the once abundant fisheries. The river front was comprehensively redeveloped in the 1980s. In the summer months the Queen's Promenade is popular with strollers and sunbathers, and a number of pubs and restaurants have tables overlooking the river.

On the Middlesex bank Kingston Bridge is at the north-

Canoeists at Teddington Lock and Weir
(left) which controls the flow of water from
the upper non-tidal reaches of the river.

A typical Edwardian boathouse at
Kingston (right).

eastern corner of Hampton Court Park. For the next three miles the river loops around the peninsula of Hampton Court, running south-west for the first mile and a half before turning north-west. At the southern end of the loop on the south bank is the relatively unspoilt village of Thames Ditton, connected to Thames Ditton Island by an elegant suspension footbridge. On the north bank Hampton Court Park is screened by a long brick wall and thick trees at the water's edge, preventing us seeing much from the river until we come upon the south gates of the palace.

When I photographed these gates they were in the process of being gilded, and were a motley mixture of grey, black and gold. The delicate wrought iron, the work of the French craftsman Jean Tijou, is part of the extensive additions to the palace carried out in the late seventeenth century. The story of Hampton Court begins with Henry VIII's adviser, Cardinal Wolsey, who bought the site in 1514, and proceeded to build himself a residence with all the grandeur and extravagance of a royal palace; he had a staff of almost 500, and 280 rooms for guests. By the late 1520s Wolsey had fallen foul of the king. When Henry's first wife, Catherine of Aragon, failed to provide him with a son and heir, he decided to annul their marriage so that he could marry Anne Boleyn. But he needed the Church's blessing, and he wanted Wolsey, as a cardinal of the Church of Rome, to persuade the Pope to oblige. Wolsey's failure to do so led to his disgrace, and in a desperate attempt to remain in favour he presented Hampton Court to the King. Henry gladly took over the palace, but dismissed Wolsey anyway. From that moment on Hampton Court became one of

the most important royal residences in the country. Its position on the river provided easy access to the City of London, as well as the other royal palaces on the Thames: Westminster, Bridewell, Whitehall, the Tower of London and Greenwich. Over the next centuries many kings and queens left their mark here. Henry himself lavished attention on Hampton Court, keeping the park well stocked with game for the royal hunt and planting many trees and shrubs in the gardens. At first Henry lived happily at Hampton Court with Anne Boleyn, and their entwined initials can still be seen on some of the stonework, but when she failed to produce a son and heir she fell from favour and was beheaded in 1536. Her successor, Jane Seymour, died at Hampton Court shortly after giving birth to Henry's only son, Edward VI, who lived here for much of his short life. After his death in 1553, at the age of sixteen, his half-sister Mary came to the throne. She also lived at Hampton Court, where she became engaged to Philip

II of Spain, spent part of her honeymoon and waited in vain for a child before she died in 1558.

Elizabeth I came to Hampton Court the following year, and lived here in great style. She was a keen gardener and, in the time-honoured tradition of the English lady, liked to work in the gardens herself. The huge kitchens, which have recently

Most of the architectural interest at Teddington is to be found in the boathouses which line the banks. This example (above) has a half-timbered pavilion perched on a brick podium.

This riverside house at Teddington (left) has a fairy-tale roofline, complete with witch's hat over the corner tower. The conservatory or greenhouse has seen better days.

Kingston Bridge (right) was built by Edward Lapidge in the 1820s. The church of Hampton Wick, on the Middlesex side, can be seen on the right.

been reinstated, provided food for the lavish banquets, masquerades and balls which Elizabeth gave; in 1590 the Duke of Württemberg described Hampton Court as 'the most splendid and most magnificent royal palace of any that may be found in England, or indeed in any other Kingdom'. Many plays were staged in the Great Hall, the oldest Elizabethan theatre to survive; when James I succeeded Elizabeth, Inigo Jones designed a number of masques for Hampton Court. James's Queen, Anne of Denmark, for whom Inigo Jones also built the Queen's House at Greenwich (see page 14), was a keen actress, and appeared in a number of the productions.

Charles I built up a famous art collection at Hampton Court, including Mantegna's masterpiece *The Triumph of Caesar*, a series of nine canvases now shown in their own gallery at the palace. After the monarchy was overthrown during the Civil War, the victorious Parliamentarians started to sell off Hampton Court and its contents; the sale was stopped when Oliver Cromwell decided to move into the palace himself in 1651, and he lived here until his death in 1658. At the Restoration Charles II set about reviving the former glory of the palace, and bought back many of the treasures sold off during the Commonwealth. He redesigned the gardens in the new formal style he had admired while travelling in France and Holland as an exile. In 1662 Pepys described a royal procession by barge from Hampton Court to Whitehall: 'Anon came the King and Queene in a barge under a canopy, with ten thousand barges and boats I think, for we could see no water for them'. Four years later, during the outbreak of the plague, the court moved to Hampton Court for safety. Charles's

brother, James II, never lived at Hampton Court; his brief reign was ended by the Glorious Revolution of 1688, when he was replaced by William and Mary.

William and Mary embarked on an ambitious building programme. William, who suffered from asthma, particularly liked the clean air at Hampton Court; the prevailing westerly winds carried the smoke and smells of London and the City in the opposite direction. Sir Christopher Wren was commissioned to build a more modern palace; at first he wanted to pull down almost all the Tudor buildings and replace them with a new scheme to rival the French king's palace at Versailles. Fortunately, he demolished only Henry VIII's State Apartments. The core of the Wren rebuilding is Fountain Court, around which he built four magnificent ranges inspired by the French Renaissance style. The south range looks towards the Thames, and a few chimneys from the Tudor buildings can be seen to the left. The block is four storeys high and twenty-five bays long. The three central bays are of Portland stone, the rest of the façade is red brick with stone dressings, and carved swags and over-windows enliven the design. One of the most distinctive features is the bull's eye windows on the third floor, like so many ship's portholes. Wren employed several great craftsmen at Hampton Court: besides Tijou's ironwork, there is Grinling Gibbons's magnificent wood carving in the Gallery and the Chapel, and Antonio Verrio's splendid illusionistic murals on the King's Staircase.

Some of this work was carried out in the reign of Queen Anne, who particularly enjoyed hunting in the park. When stricken

by gout she had a special one-horse carriage made for stag hunting, in which she raced round the grounds for hours at a time. The first two Hanoverian kings were often at Hampton Court, particularly in the summer months during the hunting season, but George III disliked the place, apparently because as a boy his grandfather, George I, had boxed his ears in the State Apartments. He preferred the palace at Kew. Although succeeding monarchs regularly visited Hampton Court, none of them lived here. Queen Victoria opened it to the public a few days a week, and in 1851 Hampton Court passed from the Crown to the Government. In 1986 a fire devastated Wren's south wing, which can be seen from the river; the extensive damage took six years to repair. The park and gardens at Hampton Court retain much of the formal planting carried out during the Stuart period: in the park three avenues of limes radiate away from the palace to the east, with a long canal down the centre avenue. The buildings are surrounded by parterres and gravel paths, and there is a knot garden as well as the famous maze, where one of Jerome K. Jerome's *Three Men in a Boat* gets helplessly lost.

One of the treasures of Hampton Court is the astronomical clock made for Henry VIII in 1540. By calculating the relative movements of the sun and the moon, the clock was able to predict the state of the tides – a very important consideration for a monarch wanting to travel to one of his other palaces on the river. Getting to Westminster or Greenwich in the royal barge would have been slow going against a rising tide, but it would be an easy matter if the journey was timed to concide with an ebb tide.

Enjoying the Thames

A variety of passenger services operate on the river. Visitors to *The Millennium Experience* at Greenwich can catch boats direct to the Dome from piers in central London and Historic Greenwich. As of 1999, public transport boats operate between Westminster and Greenwich, with stops at a number of piers in between. River trips catering for tourists include the area covered by this book, from the Thames Barrier and Greenwich in the east to Kew and Hampton Court in the west. These run mostly from the spring to the autumn, with a few winter services. There are also floating restaurants and night clubs: some are permanently moored; others travel up and down the river. An evening cruise is a particularly good way to enjoy the Thames. There are excellent riverside pubs, many with interesting historical associations with the river.

Keen oarsmen can join one of the many rowing clubs along the river; most of these are between Putney and Kew. On a more casual basis, rowing boats can be hired at Richmond Bridge during the summer months.

Walkers will want to explore the recently opened Thames Path, which runs all the way from the river's source in the depths of Gloucestershire to the Thames Barrier – a total length of 288 kilometres (180 miles). For most of its length in London it covers both banks of the Thames. Occasionally there are obstacles along the route and it has to leave the river's edge, but there are clear signs showing the way. An admirable guidebook is the *National Trail Guide to the Thames Path* by David Sharp.

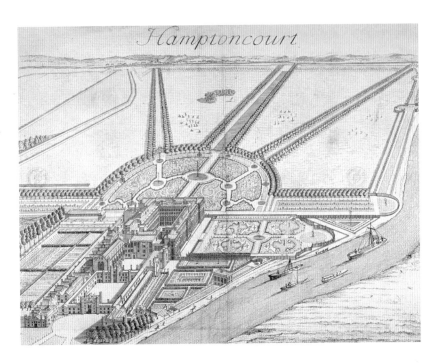

This eighteenth-century engraving (left) shows the radiating avenues and formal gardens at Hampton Court. Tijou's gates can be seen at the water's edge.

Hampton Court Palace (right) is seen through Jean Tijou's beautiful wrought iron gates. They are part of the extensive additions to the palace carried out under Christopher Wren in the late seventeenth century. The south range of his Fountain Court (red brick and Portland stone) looks towards the Thames, and chimneys from the earlier Tudor buildings can be seen to the left.

Bibliography

Dickens's Dictionary of the Thames Charles Dickens & Evans, 1893

Ordnance Survey Guide to the River Thames London: Nicholson/Ordnance Survey, 1994

The River Thames Teddington to Southend Huntingdon: Imray Charts

Barker, Felix and Peter Jackson, *History of London in Maps* London: Barrie & Jenkins, 1990

Barton, Nicholas, *The Lost Rivers of London* London: Historical Publications, 1992

Batey, Buttery, Lambert & Wilkie, *Arcadian Thames* Barn Elms, 1992

Beard, Geoffrey, *The Work of Christopher Wren* Edinburgh: John Bartholomew & Son, 1982

Blomfield, David, *Kew Past* Sussex: Phillimore, 1994

Bolland, R. R., *Victorians on the Thames* Kent: Parapress, 1994

Burford, E. J., *The Bishop's Brothels* London: Robert Hale, 1993

Clegg, Gillian, *Chiswick Past* London: Historical Publications, 1995

Cloake, John, *Richmond Past* London: Historical Publications, 1991

Clout, Hugh, *The Times London History Atlas* London: Times Books, 1991

Conrad, Joseph, *Heart of Darkness* 1910

Currie, Ian, *Frosts, Freezes and Fairs* Surrey: Frosted Earth, 1996

de Maré, Eric, *London's Riverside* London: Max Reinhardt, 1958

Dickens, Charles, *Our Mutual Friend* 1864–5

Doré, Gustave and Blanchard Jerrold, *A London Pilgrimage* London: Grant & Co, 1877

Ebel, Suzanne and Doreen Impey, *A Guide to London's Riverside* London: Constable, 1985

Gerhold, Dorian, *Putney and Roehampton Past* London: Historical Publications, 1994

Hardingham, Samantha, *London: A Guide to Recent Architecture* Cologne: Könemann, 1996

Hatts, Leigh, *The Thames Path* Cumbria: Cicerone Press, 1988

Hibbert, Christopher, *London* London: Penguin Books, 1980

Holme, Thea, *Chelsea* London: Hamish Hamilton, 1972

Inwood, Stephen, *A History of London* London: Macmillan, 1998

Jones, Edward and Christopher Woodward, *Guide to the Architecture of London* London: Weidenfeld & Nicolson, 1992

Keates, Jonathan, *Handel, the Man and his Music* London: Victor Gollancz, 1985

Linebaugh, Peter, *The London Hanged* London: Penguin, 1991

Mayhew, Henry, *London Labour and the London Poor* London: Charles Griffin, 1850s

Milne, Gustav, *Port of Roman London* London: Batsford, 1993

Palmer, Kenneth Nicholls *Ceremonial Barges on the River Thames* London: Unicorn Press, 1997

Pepys, Samuel, *Diary and Correspondence*, London: J. M. Dent, 1899

Piper, David, *Artists' London* London: Weidenfeld & Nicolson, 1982

Piper, David, *Companion Guide to London* London: HarperCollins, 1996

Porter, Roy, *London: A Social History* London: Hamish Hamilton/Penguin Books, 1994

Pudney, John, *London's Docks* London: Thames & Hudson, 1975

Room, Adrian, *Dictionary of Place-Names in the British Isles* London: Bloomsbury Publishing, 1988

Russell, John, *London* New York, NY: Harry N. Abrams, 1994

Sharp, David, *The Thames Path* London: Aurum Press, 1997

Smollett, Tobias, *The Adventures of Roderick Random* 1748

Sobel, Dava, *Longitude* London: Fourth Estate, 1996

Tames, Richard, *City of London Past* London: Historical Publications, 1995

Uglow, Jenny, *Hogarth* London: Faber & Faber, 1997

Waters, Tony, *Bridge by Bridge through London* Kent: Pryor Publications, 1989

Weightman, Gavin, *London River* London: Collins & Brown, 1990

Weinreb, Ben and Christopher Hibbert, *The London Encyclopaedia* London: Macmillan, 1993

Williams, Stephanie, *Docklands* London: Phaidon Press, 1993

Woolf, Virginia, *The London Scene* London: The Hogarth Press, 1975

The royal palace of Placentia, Henry VIII's birthplace, once stood on the site of the Royal Naval Hospital at Greenwich.

Index

S. Pa

Hamsted Mills

the Water house

Hamsted

S Brides

Baynard Castle

Pauls Warse

Quene hithe

Thre

The Fall Schipes

THAMES

The Bear Gardne